BOOK II

UNLEASH
Her

The Next Chapter Begins

HANNA OLIVAS
Along With 21 Inspiring Authors

ISBN: 978-1-968061-42-5

TABLE OF CONTENTS

INTRODUCTION

The Next Chapter Begins Now

There comes a moment in every woman's life when she feels the quiet nudge—or the loud roar—that it's time for something more. More truth. More freedom. More courage. More *her*.

Unleash Her: The Next Chapter Begins was born from that moment. It's for the woman who's tired of dimming her light, second-guessing her instincts, and living by someone else's script. It's for the woman who knows, deep down, that she was made for more—and is finally ready to claim it.

This book is not here to tell you who to be. It's here to remind you who you already are.

Within these pages, you'll find real stories from women who chose to rise—sometimes trembling, often uncertain, but always determined. You'll discover powerful insights and practical tools to help you silence the noise, break through barriers, and reconnect with the fierce strength that's always been within you.

But most importantly, you'll begin to write your *next chapter*—not out of fear or pressure, but from power, clarity, and truth.

You don't need to be perfect. You don't need permission. You just need to begin.

So let this be your moment. Let this be your declaration. Turn the page—and *unleash her*.

Hanna Olivas

Founder and CEO of SHE RISES STUDIOS

https://www.linkedin.com/company/she-rises-studios/
https://www.facebook.com/sherisesstudios
https://www.instagram.com/sherisesstudios_llc/
www.SheRisesStudios.com

Author, Speaker, and Founder. Hanna was born and raised in Las Vegas, Nevada, and has paved her way to becoming one of the most influential women of 2022. Hanna is the co-founder of She Rises Studios and the founder of the Brave & Beautiful Blood Cancer Foundation. Her journey started in 2017 when she was first diagnosed with Multiple Myeloma, an incurable blood cancer. Now more than ever, her focus is to empower other women to become leaders because The Future is Female. She is currently traveling and speaking publicly to women to educate them on entrepreneurship, leadership, and owning the female power within.

Unleash Her: The Next Chapter Begins

By Hanna Olivas

There comes a moment when you stop asking for permission. A moment where the past can no longer hold the pen and the future is no longer waiting for you to be ready. That moment is now. For so long, I was the woman who dimmed her light to make others comfortable. I made myself small to survive, until I realized surviving was no longer enough. I wanted more. I wanted the truth. I wanted to finally meet the woman I was becoming. And she was waiting on the other side of fear. Unleashing her wasn't a single act; it was a daily decision to stop living by the expectations others placed on me. It was a decision to peel off the masks, let go of the noise, and stand fully in my truth, flaws, faith, fire, and all. I've lived through storms I never signed up for. I've been abandoned, misunderstood, overlooked, and underestimated. I've lost people, lost parts of myself, and nearly lost my life. I've walked through the pain of illness, betrayal, heartbreak, and exhaustion so deep it made me question if I could keep going. But I didn't just survive. I rebuilt.

"Sometimes, the most powerful thing a woman can do is choose herself loudly, unapologetically, and without waiting for someone else to approve."

The world doesn't always know what to do with a woman who's no longer afraid to take up space. We get called names. We get labeled "too much" or "not enough." But the truth is, when you start walking in your power, people will either rise with you or remove themselves. And either way, you keep rising. I want to speak directly to the woman reading this who feels like she's stuck in the in-between. The woman who knows there's more inside her but doesn't know where to begin. The one who has been strong for everyone else, and now she's tired, wondering when it will be her turn. This is your turn. This is your next chapter. And it won't look like the old ones. You don't need to go back to who you were before the world tried to break you. You get to go forward into who you're becoming. The healed, whole, unleashed version of you. The one who doesn't just dream, but builds. The one who doesn't just endure, but embodies joy. The one who leads, loves, creates, and lives fully, even when it's messy, even when it's hard. "Unleashing her means knowing you are the fire, the storm, and the calm after it. You are not broken. You are breaking free." We were never meant to live in survival mode. But for so long, we did. We carried the weight of everyone else's expectations while burying our own dreams. We said yes when we wanted to scream no. We silenced ourselves because we were taught that a quiet woman is a good one. But I'm here to remind you that you don't owe anyone your silence. The next chapter doesn't require perfection. It requires presence. It requires truth. It requires the courage to show up as the real you, the woman who has scars and still smiles. The one who cries in the car but gets out and shows up anyway. The one who's afraid and still says yes. That's who I am. That's who you are. That's who we are. I've made a decision that I hope you'll make, too: I will no longer shrink to fit into spaces I was meant to redesign. Let this be your permission slip, your wake-up call, your invitation to stop settling and start becoming. You are not too late. You are not too broken. You are exactly on time to write the next chapter—with boldness, beauty, and belief in yourself like never before. This chapter is not about having it all figured out. It's about finally choosing to begin. And here's the truth that no one can take from you: The moment you unleash her, the powerful, messy, radiant, real woman inside of you, your life will never be the same. The next chapter begins now. And this time, it's yours.

DK Hillard

Founder of DK Hillard Art, LLC
Artist/Designer/Author

https://www.linkedin.com/in/debra-hillard-93526913/
https://www.facebook.com/dkhillardwraptures/
https://www.instagram.com/dkhillard/
https://www.dkhillard.com
https://www.dkhillardart.com

DK Hillard is a creative visionary, Priestess, and Sacred guide whose work bridges the seen and unseen. With over 20 years of experience as a trainer and life coach, she helped countless individuals transform their lives through physical training. Today, she channels her expertise into the soul realm, using both painting and fabric to create sacred, intention-infused works that invite deep reflection and transformation. As the creator of Soul Wraptures, spellwoven textiles designed to awaken the soul, and Soul Portraits, intuitive paintings that reflect the essence of one's spirit, she offers tools for remembrance and self-discovery. Her work is an invitation to connect with hidden truths, reclaim your power, and embrace your unique path. Through her writing and art, she guides others on a journey of healing, awakening, and personal transformation. Everything she creates is a ritual, a prayer, a reflection — for those walking the path of deep remembering.

Breaking the Chains: A Spiritual Journey of Liberation Across Lifetimes

By DK Hillard

Early November 2024. A year had passed since my first Shamanic ceremony—an experience that irrevocably altered the course of my life. That year had been one of profound transformation. I had written a book, accelerated the evolution of my business, and believed I was well on my way to becoming my truest self. The world felt like it had opened wide before me, and I stood at the threshold of a life I had always imagined. But despite all that I had gained, something essential remained missing. I knew, deep within, that the only way to uncover it was to plunge deeper into the unknown.

With the knowledge of who I had become came the haunting emptiness that had long lingered, a shadow over my soul. I felt chained, bound to an unseen force that imprisoned parts of me I could not name. This missing fragment of myself had been held captive for so many lifetimes, its prison had become a part of me. I had no clear vision of what it would take to sever those bonds, but one truth was certain: I was on the path to reclaiming it.

With each layer of myself that I uncovered, with each moment of personal growth, there was this sense of a haunting emptiness—an echo from deep within, almost as if something had been trapped in me for generations. It was as though a hidden piece of me, a fragment of my soul, was imprisoned in some unseen cage and I had no idea where to find the key.

Although my spirit had returned in profound ways, there remained parts of me locked away, held captive by something beyond my current awareness. For years, I had lived with that lingering feeling—of being almost whole but not entirely, of knowing there was more, something that needed to be unearthed. The invisible chains that bound me were not tangible, not something I could touch or name, yet I knew they were there, restricting me in ways that I could not fully grasp. I had to dig deeper.

The woman I was before my first ceremony no longer existed, replaced by someone who was becoming increasingly attuned to the mysteries of the spirit world. The woman I had been, the one I refer to as my "mother," was the version of myself who had surrendered her life fully to a greater purpose. She had stepped into the role of service, surrendering the personal desires of the ego to serve the greater truth of Spirit. This was the woman who devoted her life to freeing herself, and ultimately freeing me, to walk this earth in truth. I was walking the same path she did, but there was more—much more—yet to be revealed. Now, it was my turn to complete the process. I knew the path I had to walk, but I did not know where it would lead or how it would unfold. I was blind again, unsure of what lay ahead, but deeply aware that I had to follow this calling.

As a Priestess, fully devoted to my spiritual path, I understood that the answers I sought would not be found in the physical realm. This was not about achieving more, accomplishing more, or attaining more recognition. It was a deeper journey—one that could only unfold through surrender.

The surrender I experienced during my last ceremony in September 2023 was monumental. But I knew this time would be different. It would require a surrender of a far greater magnitude, something that would shake me to my core. So, after a year of integrating the realizations from my first ceremony, I returned to my sacred tree and prepared to drink the brew that would unlock the doors of my soul once again.

With each ceremony, Spirit had asked me for something—a request, a question to guide the unfolding. I had always been given what I needed, but this time, I asked for something specific. This time, I asked to be set free from the invisible chains that held me back from living my fullest truth. I asked to be unburdened from the weight of lifetimes of fears and trauma, to shed the layers that had accumulated over the centuries and find out who I truly was beneath it all. No matter the cost, I was ready. The time had come. I was ready for my freedom and willing to do whatever was required of me to see this through.

Unlike my first journey, which unfolded in the quiet stillness of night, this one began in the full light of day. Sunlight streamed through the canopy of leaves above me, casting intricate patterns on the ground, as if the universe itself had decided to step forward and bear witness. The air around me was crisp, and I could feel the autumn chill in my bones. The world seemed real and sharp, present in ways that were both comforting and unnerving. It was a moment that asked for clarity. As I lay beneath the tree, I could hear the hum of the world around me. It wasn't a distraction; it was a reminder that everything was connected, and that I, too, was a part of this great, living web. And in this sacred moment, I asked my guide to light the fire.

The fire, which had always been a symbol of purification and transformation, felt more intense than ever before. The warmth it offered was welcome at first, but quickly became an unbearable agony. It felt as though the flames were not just physical—they were soul-deep, burning through the very fabric of my being. The stench of burning flesh hung heavy in the air, and in that moment, I was transported through lifetimes—each one ending at the stake, a soul condemned by persecution. The fire licked at my skin, searing my essence, burning away the layers of illusion and ego. I could feel my body dissolve, the flames pulling away the skin, the muscle, the very core of who I thought I was, as I also witnessed my body melt before my eyes. The stench of burning flesh filled my nostrils, sickening and too real. It was not a new sensation. I had experienced this in visions before, in memories of past lives that were so vivid they felt as if they had just happened. I had felt the flames in my soul long before they touched my skin. It was an agony that seemed endless. The pain seemed to stretch on for eternity, each moment a new iteration of suffering, as though the fire had no intention of stopping.

For what felt like forever, I experienced the depth of this torment. I did not know if it would end in death—whether I would be consumed in this flame like so many versions of myself had been in past lives. I could feel my consciousness stretching, reaching the edge of its limits, and yet the fire remained. Then, as suddenly as it had begun, the flames receded, and something shifted.

I was no longer surrounded by fire. Now, I was encased in stone. I could feel the weight of the earth pressing down on me, the crushing mass of rock surrounding me on all sides. I was trapped in this living tomb, a prisoner within the walls of my own creation. But there was no escape through death, no release from the agony. The stone pressed down, layer after layer, each one sealing me deeper into this inescapable place. I was suffocated by the weight of time itself, unaware of how long I had been there or how much longer I would remain. Beyond time, beyond space, I existed solely within this moment of confinement.

It was a prison I had built for myself, one I could not escape from. I was cut off from the world, cut off from the light, from life itself. Without time, I felt an eternity of isolation, both from others and from my own life. Yet, in the midst of this tomb, there was a subtle shift. I began to feel heat once again. It wasn't the fire I had known; this heat seemed to be coming from deep within me. I was the fire now. My very energy was becoming the heat that burned brighter and brighter, even though I could see no visible source.

The light that radiated from within me blazed. I opened my eyes to see if it was outside, but the daylight had waned and there was no more sunlight streaking through the branches. Night had arrived and with it, an unbearably blinding light emanating from my core. And though the stone continued to press down on me, I no longer felt trapped. The heat of my energy, the power within me, was stronger than the stone. The walls around me cracked, then shattered, until there was nothing left to contain me. In a moment I was free.

And then, in a surge of energy, I was flying. I was a fire-breathing dragon, soaring through the sky, wild and free, dancing among the stars, completely untethered. The feeling was like nothing I had ever known before. I could feel the ecstasy of liberation, the freedom of movement, of being unbound by any limitation. It was as if my root chakra had ignited, fueling me with primal energy, grounding me to the Earth while allowing me to reach beyond the stars. I was unchained, unrestrained, completely and utterly liberated.

Does it sound like a fantasy? Maybe it does, but this was not a fantasy. This was real. It was the culmination of lifetimes of work, of healing, of growth. It was the return of my soul to itself. The fire, once external, was now my own, and in that moment, I felt the raw, untamed power of what it means to truly be unleashed. But as much as it was a moment of profound ecstasy, it was also a moment of reckoning. This freedom, this power, came with a responsibility. The soul that had been freed now had to be embodied. The truth I had uncovered needed to be lived. No longer could I hide in the shadows of my past. I had to live as the person I had become.

And so, my journey continues, but now it is not one of seeking or searching. It is one of embodying what has been found. The mandate from Spirit was clear: I am a healer. I have been given the responsibility to step fully into that role and help others unlock their truth. But I do not walk alone. I walk alongside others, as a fellow traveler, not as someone who has it all figured out, but as someone who is still learning, still growing, and still walking the path toward deeper truth. Each step is a practice, a prayer, a devotion to living fully in alignment with Spirit.

Living as an embodied truth is not an easy task. I have spent a lifetime preparing for this moment, yet that does not make this part of the journey any less challenging. The difference now is that I walk forward with more faith in myself, in the path I have chosen, and in the guidance that surrounds me. Although I may still feel blind at times, I trust in the whispers that come from within, in the guidance that is not outside of me but an integral part of my own essence. This is the new way forward—the way of integration, of balancing the spiritual with the physical, of living as an embodied Priestess.

My body, though a vessel for my spirit, has been through much in this lifetime. It is worn, scarred, and tested by the battles of survival, of being human. I know that this body was never meant to contain the full magnitude of my soul. And yet, I agreed to this. I accepted it. But now, as I grow older, I feel the constraints of this vessel more acutely. The question that arises is, how does the fire of a dragon fit into a body that can no longer fly at warp speed? How does this vast energy find a way to live, to express itself, without consuming the very vessel it inhabits?

And what does embodiment look like for a Priestess whose energy is so vast, so fierce, that it threatens to ignite everything in its path? This is the question I am learning to answer. I am learning to channel this fire, to live with it, to express it in ways that do not overwhelm, but rather uplift, heal, and inspire, not only others, but myself.

I know who I am now.

I am Priestess, I am Shaman, I am Warrior, I am Witch.

I am a creator, a vessel through which magic and miracles flow. I am here to offer healing, to guide others on their own path to truth and freedom. I have come to understand that my path is not only about finding my truth, but also helping others discover theirs. I am a living bridge between the worlds, a connector of the seen and the unseen, the known and the unknown.

This new chapter is the one my "mother" longed for—the freedom to live fully as herself, unbound by the limitations of predestined beliefs and patterns. I, too, long to embrace that freedom, but find myself in unfamiliar territory. The vision of freedom that I once had belongs to a younger version of myself, one who was more vigorous, more agile. And yet, I know that even though my body may feel worn, even though I may feel fatigued, the fire within me is as potent as ever, perhaps more so. It is my work to create channels for this immense energy that will help my body heal while helping others along their own path.

And so, I continue on this journey, one step at a time, trusting that each moment, each choice, brings me closer to the freedom I seek. As I embrace my own truth, I do so with the awareness that my choices ripple out into the world, affecting not only my life but the lives of those around me. The path of the Priestess is not an easy one, but it is the one I have chosen, the one my soul has been called to walk.

I know who I am. And with that knowing comes the responsibility to live it, fully and without apology.

Feeling inspired by what you've just read and ready to explore further? I offer a transformative process to help you reconnect with the truth of who you are, creating unique and powerful anchors through my art. Reach out to me here to start your journey.

Hunyah Irfan

HunyahTravels
Content Creator

https://www.linkedin.com/in/hunyah-irfan-blogger351/?originalSubdomain=ca
https://www.facebook.com/OfficialHunyahTravels
https://www.instagram.com/officalhunyahtravels/
https://ca.linkedin.com/in/hunyah-irfan-blogger351

Hunyah is a content creator with a background in community development. You can find Hunyah doing food reviews , interviewing people and more. Hunyah is actively involved in the community for different events.

Unleash Your Creativity

By Hunyah Irfan

Hi Everyone,

I'm Hunyah and I'm from Brampton, Ontario. I'm here to talk about ways of unleashing your creativity. Not everyone is a content creator but there are many things you can do on a regular basis to unleash your creativity.

These are some of the ways you can unleash your creativity:

1. Mixed Media
2. Writing
3. Dance
4. Meditation

Mixed Media

Mixed media is not just for filming. It is also for creating works with craft tools on the canvas.

That can be like what little kids do, making sculptures with newspapers or Styrofoam.

You don't need to be a professional artist for this.

It involves using different materials to create different pieces.

This is a way of unleashing your creativity. That is good for health.

That is because it's a way to take out the stress, and it helps release stress from your body.

I would say that is an art therapy.

Writing

As a kid, I loved to write, and I still write until now.

Writing is a good way to let your depression, pain, or anything that puts you down into poetry.

As a spoken word artist, the creative writing process gets better each time.

This gives a way to unleash your depression.

Additionally, this allows you to improve your vocabulary.

This gets the writer to use new words in the poetry.

As well as Googling the words.

This helps develop strong writing skills.

Also, this is important in business writing skills.

That is why creative writing is another way to unleash your creativity.

Dance

Dance is a good way to exercise and stay active.

You can take training, too, for dancing, but it isn't required all the time.

That is good for health and keeps you active and keeps you fit.

Even dancing simple steps can still be beneficial for your health.

I have been dancing since I was a kid.

I have some dance training too, which I acquired over the years.

I have represented Canada in the dance division for the World Perfect Athlete 2025 competition.

I do Bollywood dance, but dancing is really good for you in many ways.

Meditation

Meditation is a way to relax and put yourself at ease.

That is because sometimes you need to be in a calm space to rest.

This lets you work on the breathing as a breathing exercise but also lets you relax.

Meditation is important when you need it.

It is a way to figure out what you need to do for yourself.

These are my tips on unleashing your creativity.

Dorothe Philippe

Dorothe Philippe
Mentor in Intuition and Telepathy

https://www.linkedin.com/in/dorothephilippe/
https://facebook.com/dorothe.philippe?locale=fr_FR
https://instagram.com/dorothe.philippe/?hl=fr
https://www.dorothephilippe.com

Dorothe is a mentor in intuition and telepathy with over twenty years of experience. Originally from Germany and living in France, she is the mother of four grown children and has been a passionate rider since childhood. Her journey began when a healer helped her family avoid a tragic fate and taught her how to access her intuition, an innate ability we all possess. Not long after, she was chosen by Volcano, a young former stunt horse who was difficult to approach. Through him, she learned how becoming more conscious of our thoughts, emotions, actions and language can help us live in alignment, achieve success and lead a joyful life. Dorothe works internationally as a life coach, animal psychologist and healer. She has co-authored several books and is committed to sharing knowledge about intuition and telepathy, empowering others to grow into their true potential.

A Course in Miracles

By Dorothe Philippe

What if Everything Is Possible?

Have you ever questioned the following:

- What if everything is possible?
- What if my dreams, desires and longings could come true?
- What if doing what I deeply yearn for is the key?
- What if I could choose the life I want to live?
- What would be the benefits of such a life?
- What could be its drawbacks?

Maybe you have not asked yourself these questions regularly, or at all. Most of us do not think in terms of miracles. We think as we were conditioned to think. This leaves us with fewer choices.

It's not that we don't believe in miracles or hope for them. Turning to the Divine, praying for help when something awful happens, when illness, financial problems, death and despair knock on our door, seems only natural and normal. Who has not done this? Yet, to the majority of people, miracles are a mystery and out of reach. And once things are good or better, it is as if they do not even exist.

How is this possible? Is the world not full of wonders? How does it come then that we do not expect them? Deep within, the longing for aliveness, growth, joy and marvel, however, never leaves us. You might silence this voice, but it remains. Life itself is a miracle. Thriving is the blueprint of the Universe, and we are part of it.

So, how about bringing more miracles into your life, not just for the next chapter or in times of crisis? Let's explore together.

Reframing Your Definition of Miracle

The word miracle comes from the old French, but its roots are Latin:

- *mirus* – wonderful
- *mirari* – to wonder and
- *miraculum* – object of wonder

This reveals something powerful and can help you to tune into the frequency you need for anything you wish for yourself, your loved ones, people or situations you want to help.

Now let's look up the definition of miracle in dictionaries. This is very interesting to do as the original meaning of a word may completely change over the centuries. Moreover, dictionaries are also a reference for general knowledge, common opinion and way of thinking. According to the Cambridge Dictionary, a miracle is "an <u>unusual</u> and <u>mysterious</u> <u>event</u> that is <u>thought</u> to have been <u>caused</u> by a <u>god</u> because it does not <u>follow</u> the <u>usual</u> <u>laws</u> of <u>nature</u>. It goes on with "a very <u>lucky</u> <u>event</u> that is <u>surprising</u> and <u>unexpected</u>." I did not search further. I found what I was looking for and how we are conditioned in terms of miracles. What intrigued me was words like unusual, mysterious, unexpected, and the statement that miracles do not follow the usual laws of nature.

Yet, life taught me the opposite.

- Miracles are natural.
- They follow the laws of nature.
- Expecting them as such may change a lot for us.

But before I go on, let me share a little about my journey into the miraculous.

About Me

I was born and raised in Germany. Before marrying my wonderful French husband, I worked for a corporate company in Munich. I then moved to Paris and became a happy, busy mother of four. Until autumn 2002, my life was not always smooth, but more or less identical to what most of us live. The day I opened the door to Michel, a healer, my whole worldview was completely shattered. A world of new possibilities emerged. In working with Michel and becoming his student for a couple of days, I discovered that reality is not limited to what we can see, hear or touch. Reality is far more expansive. And it can be changed.

Soon after, Michel died. Alone, with my new knowledge and all the questions I had, I turned to life itself for answers, using my intuition. What I had only done in difficult times before, now became a daily habit. I received messages and healing techniques from other dimensions, and over time, a different consciousness and awareness were installed.

In 2002, I also met my horse Volcano, who is now twenty-nine and enjoying his well-earned retirement. He, too, became a faithful guide and teacher. Over the years, I've had the privilege of helping many animal and human clients, yet the journey of learning is never truly complete. That's why I consider myself a lifelong student and keen observer of Life. I love sharing fresh perspectives and creating meaningful connections that bring us closer to our soul. I do this across the three languages I speak and in many corners of the world, wearing various hats: life coach, spiritual teacher, mentor in intuition and telepathy, animal psychologist and communicator, healer and author.

For more details about the beginning of my journey and how to tap into your intuition, please get a copy of the anthology *She Stands Strong* or download a free summary on my website https://www.dorothephilippe.com.

What Animals Teach Us About Miracles

Since autumn 2002, I have also been studying animals. Animals are a huge part of my world. They are very inspiring, and I love to learn from them. Animals are extremely coherent. They keep things simple and essential. They do what they want, need and desire, and they pursue it. They know their potential and give themselves the means to reach their goals. When you offer an animal healing, it accepts it fully. It won't question whether the healing will last, whether it's too good to be true or whether miracles do really exist. Animals choose to their advantage and to the common good. They act in alignment with themselves and the laws of nature. And this is how they manifest amazing outcomes.

When you work with animals, you will realize that they easily become mirrors of yourself. That's a precious gift. The human mind is a never-ending process. It is creative and serves us in many wonderful ways. The trouble is that most of what we think, believe and feel, say and do happens beyond our awareness. Dr. Bruce Lipton, American biologist and founder of Epigenetics, points out that ninety-five percent of our mind operates through habits. He calls this the habit mind. Habits happen automatically. Automatically means you are on "auto-pilot", but you do not know it.

Animals are outstanding telepathic. They have the capacity to read your thoughts and emotions. So, if I have the chance to access my unconscious mind to undo thought and belief patterns and reprogram behaviors that do not serve me and sabotage what I really want, I go for it. For more on telepathy and why your inner telepathic message counts, please refer to my chapter in *EmpowerHer: Narratives Rooted in Truth Driven by Resilience, and led by Women.* For now, let's talk about how to think more miraculously.

Quantum Entanglement and the Power of Thought

Quantum physics and neuroscience could show that our thoughts, actions, emotions and words impact our reality. In 1997, the University of Geneva, Switzerland, conducted an experiment on photons, permitting a new way of seeing the world. Photons are particles of light. Quantum physics teaches that all matter is made up of particles of light.

For the experiment, scientists had split a single photon into two, creating "twins" with identical properties. The two particles were then fired off in opposite directions. At fourteen miles from each other, at the end of their trajectory, the twins were "forced" to choose between two identical-looking random routes. The outcome was surprising: both made exactly the same choices and travelled the same path each time. Physicists called this connection *quantum entanglement.*

In an article, project leader Nicholas Gisin later explained: "What is fascinating is that the entangled photons form one and the same object. Even when the twin photons are separated geographically. If one of them is modified, the other photon automatically undergoes the same change."

The experiment confirmed what ancient teachings have told us for eons:

- All is one.
- Everything is connected.
- Thought and energy create matter.

The Teachings of Oria

Physics can be abstract. Let's become clearer about what quantum entanglement really means, how it works in our physical world and how it helps us in terms of miracles.

My friend Véronique had kittens. When they were six weeks old, her husband tripped over one. He got mad and insisted that the kittens had to go, or he would leave the house. I took one and named him Oria. When Oria was about two and a half months old, the weather was lovely and the whole family was outside. Due to his young age, I had kept Oria inside since his arrival. On this beautiful day, however, when all our other animals were with us in the garden, I felt sorry that Oria was not with us and went inside to get him. Let's analyze what happened next and what we can learn from it.

From an early age on, animal mothers leave their offspring alone as they need to hunt and feed themselves. As soon as they can, the little ones go on adventures. In general, they stay not far from their birth or hiding place and explore the environment, seeming to know when there is danger and when to get back to their hiding spot. Thanks to my studies in animal ethology, I know all this. Haven't I seen tons of scientific videos and read pages and pages of scientific publications on animal behavior for years? The trouble was, I had seen the vet before. Oria did not have all his vaccines yet, and I had been told not to let him out until he was protected as needed. Well, animals in the wild do not have vaccines. They are protected by their natural immune system, and our pets are as well. I could mentally handle that. The vet must have said something else, however, which must have conditioned me, as I did the unbelievable at least, when you look at my professional background.

All looks safe, I thought, Oria in my arms after having frantically checked my garden for danger. Our garden was huge, but was mainly surrounded by walls. This assured me. But then my eyes captured our old massive lime tree.

He must just not go on there, I concluded in putting down Oria.

What do you think the little thing did right away?

Well, Oria instantly ran to the lime tree and up he was to its top. My husband had to get his mountain ropes and climb the lime to get him down.

Okay, I thought. *I got it. Tomorrow, not one single stupid thought*, I swore to myself in reminding that thoughts and emotions create reality and that all is one. Knowing this is one thing. Mastering the conditioned mind is another.

The following day, the moment I was putting Oria down, my eyes caught the hole in the neighbor's fence. *How could I forget* rushed through my mind. Too late! Oria was already on his way. Aware of how I had triggered things the day before, I was on my way, too, just in time to catch him halfway through.

By the third day, I finally managed to focus on what I really wanted: to enjoy the sun together. I also held the right emotion: joy.

What do you think was the outcome of the story?

Well, now, Oria played around my feet or sunbathed like the whole family. As before, he was only a reflection of me. I have hundreds of stories like this to tell.

Quantum entanglement is constant. It is a natural law. If you want miracles, you must stay focused on what you desire and course-correct as needed.

Miracle-Readiness and Right Thinking

Miracles are natural. In nature, they happen all the time. If they are not happening in our lives, something is blocking them. In general, it is fear. Fear is usually the opposite of what we really want. Fear stems from wrong thinking. Miracles arise from right thinking and from a state of mind of miracle-readiness. There is more to it, but this is the essential:

- Be ready for change

- Be clear on your goal
- Set intentions
- Heart and mind open
- Take action
- Imagine and feel as if ... had already happened
- Keep focus
- Trust the process
- Observe yourself
- Correct if necessary

Most of our conditioning comes before age six or seven from family, school, culture and religion. Know, however, that anything which we hear, see or witness repetitively conditions us. So, if you want miracles, start identifying and releasing limiting beliefs.

You were given everything at birth. Your heart and your mind never lose their creative force. There is nothing about you that you cannot attain. Remind yourself that all thinking produces form at some level. So, guard your thoughts carefully.

Know that events as such are neutral. Events only obtain meaning through the way we look at them. Perception creates emotions. Emotions influence decisions. Decisions shape actions. Actions lead to results. Results create experiences. This is a cycle.

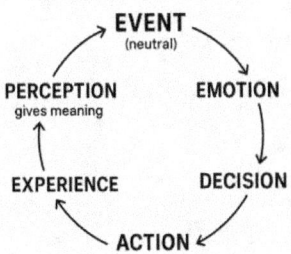

EVENTS ARE NEUTRAL. THEY OBTAIN MEANING THROUGH THE WAY WE LOOK AT THEM.

EVENT (neutral)

PERCEPTION gives meaning — EMOTION — DECISION — ACTION — EXPERIENCE

THIS IS A CYCLE.

The power to live miracles belongs to you. The key to what you experience is your perception. It controls the rest. I have designed the following image to upload for further help. Just being aware of this cycle is already extremely helpful.

Final Thoughts: Walk in Beauty

Life is wonderful. There is a marvel for us all. Walk in beauty. Keep on dreaming. Don't hesitate to call for help, whether from God, the Universe, angels, nature, your intuition or anyone or anything close to your heart. Make the best you can out of your life. You have everything you need inside.

Now, take a last moment as you are still in the energy of what you have just read, and ask yourself the following:

- What is one belief I hold that might limit me?
- What are the benefits of this belief? How does this serve me?
- What are its drawbacks? How does this serve me?

You can answer the questions from above as those below in two ways:

- Rapidly, from the place of your intuition, in noting the first thing that comes up, or
- In taking your time and coming from the place of your rational mind.

Do this on a regular basis and for all areas of your life. See what happens.

If ever you feel stuck, please feel free to reach out.

Wishing you luck and as many miracles as possible,
Dorothe

https://www.dorothephilippe.com/
https://www.linkedin.com/in/dorothephilippe/
https://facebook.com/dorothe.philippe?locale=fr_FR
https://instagram.com/dorothe.philippe/?hl=fr

Hannah Darby GMBPsP SMACCPH

Healing with Hannah
Holistic Healer and Grief Therapist

https://www.linkedin.com/in/hannahdarbyhealingwithhannah/
https://www.facebook.com/hannahsdarby
https://www.instagram.com/healingwithhannahd/
https://www.healingwithhannah.co.uk/
https://www.accph.org.uk/united-kingdom/martley/therapists-
and-coaches/hannah-darby

Hannah Darby GMBPsP SMACCPH is an award winning trauma and grief therapist who helps guide individuals on their personal grief journey. Hannah's unique Kintsgui Method with H.E.A.L approach has been featured in the international magazines, She Wins and Becoming an Unstoppable Woman. Hannah is a General Member of the British Psychological Society, a Senior Member of Accredited Counsellors, Coaches, Psychotherapists and Hypnotherapists, a Reiki Master, a HeartHealing® practitioner, Masseuse and an International Bestselling Author. Hannah runs Healing with Hannah, a unique therapy practice based on her professional and personal wisdom guided by science and spirituality. Hannah guides people on their personal grief journeys with care and compassion. Hannah works with your mind, heart and body to help you find deep healing with soulful integration. Hannah resides in the British countryside with her husband, four cats and two chihuahuas. Hannah loves heavy metal, horror movies and country walks.

Unleash Your Grief, Unleash Your Power

By Hannah Darby GMBPsP SMACCPH

We so often look outside of ourselves for the answers to our deepest questions, for guidance on what to do, where to go and how to get there. Yet more often than not, the answer lies within us. We are just too blind, scared or unaware of how to find it. But by digging deep and taking the first steps on your healing journey, you can start to uncover your hidden gifts and talents. You can unleash your power within.

In order to unleash your power, you have to dig deep into the darkest parts of your soul and face your inner demons lurking within the shadows. We all have different demons to face. However, they are all built upon the same limiting beliefs, which are manifested through different events or traumas in our lives. It is within these shadows that your limiting beliefs lie, all the parts of yourselves we have been taught to bury, or are ashamed to bring into the light. Limiting beliefs are any beliefs that hold you back, stopping you from achieving what you desire. These thoughts and feelings you have nurtured based upon the darkest moments in your life's journey. Thoughts like *I'm not good enough, I'm not smart enough, I'm not pretty enough, I'm not capable, I don't deserve this...* Often, your greatest gifts and your greatest powers are buried deep within these shadows. We look at others who seem to have it all, not realising that we all think and feel this way at some point in our lives, and we all have our own limiting beliefs. Unleashing your power is about not letting these parts of your soul control you; you must face them and then take control of them. Show them that you are in control of you, and no matter what happens, they cannot dim your light. You will shine brightly for the world to see, regardless of what life throws at you.

Your limiting beliefs are often formed in childhood by the experiences you have gone through. Once you form a belief, your brain looks for things to support this belief, feeding into the warped native of your mind. Rewriting these beliefs means facing the situation that made them, and more often than not, those are experiences you don't want to revisit, or you don't even realise this is where they came from. Experiences and traumatic events that your brain has buried to protect you. At the time, this serves a purpose, but as time goes on, it holds you back and stops you from unleashing your power within. It takes time, courage, perseverance and a want for change, a want for something more than the pain you feel within. For me, some of my worst limiting beliefs came from a life lived in grief, lost in the darkness of depression, the chains of anxiety and a willingness to feel anything but the pain inside. As time goes on, these beliefs seed themselves deep within your mind. You have to have the strength to pull them out by the root. You have to face your fears, walk into the shadows, turn on the light and take back what is rightfully yours.

Healing yourself uncovers your path to unleashing your inner power and gifts. Healing isn't easy. It isn't pretty. It takes courage, resilience and perseverance. Healing is by no means the easy path to take. It is the raw, uncensored part of yourself. It means facing the darkest moments of your life head-on, feeling those emotions but not holding on to them. You have to have the strength to go into the dark shadows of your soul and find the light. Most importantly, you have to show yourself care and compassion along the way.

I often think of healing like an onion. As soon as you work on one layer, there is always another layer underneath. It's an eternal cycle. It is a common misconception that you can be fully healed. No one is truly healed. There are always more layers to go through, more healing to be done. Healing is a continual journey, and one that you cannot do alone. Asking for help is difficult, especially if you have experienced some form of trauma. This gives you a need to have to do it alone, masking itself as independence. A little independence is good, but a lot of independence holds us back, as we all have different strengths and weaknesses. You need someone to guide you through your weakest parts. You can feel as though asking for help is weak, yet in fact, it is a form of strength. Recognising when and where you need assistance takes courage that few people have. Unfortunately, there are many people out there who do not admit to their shadows, who are unwilling to face their demons, yet still claim to be able to help others.

Any form of inner work takes courage; if you are on this path, then give yourself the credit you deserve. The first step is always the hardest to take. Whatever you have been through. Whatever you are going through. Whatever is to come, know that you are worthy of healing, worthy of success, worthy of finding the inner peace we all crave, worthy of unleashing your power within.

The thing that truly kept me from unleashing my power was grief. We all experience grief at some point in our lives; some experience it more than others, but it is something you cannot escape. Grief has many different faces and various ways in which it can enter your life that go far beyond life and death. Grief is a complex set of emotions that you go through when you experience any form of loss, the loss of anything that was important to you. The sooner you embrace your grief, the sooner you can unleash your power within it.

Many people have studied grief. Do you recognise yourself in any of these theories? Sigmund Freud discussed the melancholy in mourning and the effect it has on the ego struggling to accept the reality of what was lost. Mourning is what you do on the outside, whereas grief is what is going on inside of us, that part that no one else sees.

Elizabeth Kübler-Ross described the stages of grief as a cycle that we go through repeatedly. Each time you go round, the cycle gets a little easier to manage. But you may not go through the cycle in the order she suggested. However, at some point in your grief journey, you will experience all of these:

- Denial,

- Anger,
- Bargaining,
- Depression,
- Acceptance.

David Kessler added a sixth stage to this cycle—Meaning. Finding the meaning in your grief is a powerful thing to do.

John Bowlby used the attachment theory to explain grief. He explained that the nature of your grief depends on the type of attachment you had with what you lost. He described four stages:

1. Shock and Numbness,
2. Yearning and Searching,
3. Disorganisation and Despair,
4. Reorganisation.

Therese Rando talked of the Six R's of mourning, the signs of grief you express on the outside:

1. Recognize and acknowledge the loss,
2. React to the separation,
3. Recollect and Re-experience the loss and its relationship,
4. Relinquish old attachments,
5. Readjust to your new world,
6. Reinvest your emotional energy into new goals.

J. William Worden spoke of the four tasks of grief. These four tasks you go through in order to understand your grief:

1. To accept the reality of your loss,
2. To work through the pain,
3. To adjust to your new environment,
4. To emotionally relocate the lost and move forward with life.

It is important to know of these, as each theory has its own value. Each one gives you hope for the future and the courage to carry on.

Not one theory stands alone; they form an understanding of your grief so that you may stop being consumed by it. By applying all the above theories, you can start to make sense of your grief, start to unleash your grief, and thereby unleash your power buried within it.

Grief is something you are taught to hide, taught to bury deep within you. Perhaps due to a fear of being seen as weak, matched with a lack of understanding and compassion from those around you. Yet you need to unleash your grief in order to heal. Healing is the path to unleashing your power. Grief gives us empathy and compassion; it teaches us about the world, about the infinite cycle of life. It gives us a deeper appreciation for the good things, the little wins: watching the sunrise, walking in nature, embracing every smile moment in your life with both hands. Grief is not something to be scared of but rather something to embrace, as grief is rooted in love. A love for what we lost. It is within love that your greatest powers lie. Your love for others, love for yourself, love for your faith and love for your environment.

We all walk the path of grief, but it is a deeply personal experience. There is no right or wrong way to grieve; your way is right for you. Time does not heal grief; time can become your enemy if you don't embrace your grief. Grief is not linear; it has no logic, and it enters every part of your existence. If you try to fight against it, you will never win. You have to learn to live with it. It doesn't leave you, but rather becomes a part of who you are. Grief changes you, and you can never go back to who you were beforehand. Facing this fact takes courage.

I have lived my whole adult life in grief, yet I did not recognise this until just a few years ago. I grieve for my lost relatives: my grandparents, my aunty, and most notably my father, who died suddenly when I was just 13. I grieve for friends I made along the way who are no longer with us. I grieve for lost parts of myself after a life-changing car accident where I broke my back, leaving me in pain. I grieve for the present and future I lost when I developed ME/CFS. I grieve for the environment, for the climate emergency we have put the Earth in. This grief fed into the limiting beliefs formed from decades of bullying; it buried the best parts of me. In fact, it almost killed me. However, I have emerged emotionally stronger and much more resilient than I was before, able to appreciate life through fresh eyes, able to use my pain to help serve others. For this, I am eternally grateful to my grief; without it, I would not be the powerful woman I am today.

Yet it has given me more than I ever expected. It has fueled my kindness, my compassion, my empathy. It fueled my passion for learning, leading me to study psychology at university. It led me on a path to searching for spiritual enlightenment. It made my faith in God stronger than it ever was before. It showed me a path towards healing modalities I found so useful, I trained in them myself, including Reiki and HeartHealing™.

My grief made me who I am today. Unleashing my grief unleashed my power within, my gift of guiding others along their personal grief journeys. You have to express your grief, not repress it, in order to H.E.A.L.

- H: Heal your relational wounds
- E: Express your pain and anger
- A: Accept your new reality
- L: Learn to love and live again

This is the backbone of my therapy work. I walk with you along the path of your own personal grief journey, like a guiding light in the dark. I hold your hand whilst you face your shadows, slay your inner demons and find the purpose buried within your pain. You have to feel your grief, feel and explore all your emotions within that grief, then allow them to pass. Holding on to them causes you nothing but heartache.

Following this myself has helped me accept who I am, and it has allowed me to embrace myself. To truly feel worthy of success. It allowed me to accept my new reality and live life to the fullest, letting love lead the way. This has unleashed my power within, giving me clarity and purpose to my life. It has enabled me to see the world from a different point of view. It has helped me to appreciate all the little things in life, for all of those little things add up to the big things.

Facing my grief and unleashing my power has opened me up to more opportunities than I ever could have dreamed of. I have won an award for my therapy practice, recognizing my work in inspiring others. HeartHealing™ is a multi-award-winning therapy that I am proud to deliver. I have become an international bestselling author, sharing my story to inspire others and give them the strength that they need to unleash their own power. I run my own healing business, Healing with Hannah, guiding clients along their own personal grief journeys. All of this is down to the fact that I have faced the shadows in my soul, tamed the demons hiding within them and shone my light regardless of what happens. I have unleashed my power within, and it feels incredible!

Your power lies within you. It is not something to be found externally, but something you must find internally—something you must have the will to search for. It is found inside the darkest depths of your soul. You must have the courage to find it and release it. Society wants you to keep this power buried, as they strive to control you, brainwash you into accepting their reality as it is. But by questioning your life, your pain and your struggles, you can learn to thrive, no matter what happens. Having that inner strength enables you to face any challenge life throws at you. It allows you to question life and find the lessons in each experience. It allows you to heal from whatever trauma you have faced, knowing that nothing can stop you now. No matter what you go through, your shining light cannot be extinguished. You are stronger than you realise, far more capable than you can imagine, more resilient than you give yourself credit for, and far more caring than you realise. Once you have mastered this, you can unleash your power within. There is no stopping you now; you can create miracles in your life. This is what it means to unleash her.

Sonya McDonald

Founder and CEO of Sonya McDonald LLC

https://www.linkedin.com/in/sonya-mcdonald-rn-bsn-bcc-7786521b9/
https://www.facebook.com/sonya.mcdonald.96
https://www.instagram.com/sonyamcdonald_/
https://www.sonyamcdonald.com

Sonya McDonald is a much sought-after expert as a Board-Certified Transformational Life Coach, Author, Speaker, and Registered Nurse with 30 years of experience. She received her Board Certification as a Life Coach from Robbins Madanes Training Institute, the official coach training school of Tony Robbins. She dedicates her life to empowering women to conquer fear, rise above overwhelm, confidently embracing a life of authenticity and fulfillment. Living with Rheumatoid Arthritis and Fibromyalgia for over 16 years, and anxiety since childhood, Sonya proves that chronic and invisible illness does not define you. When she's not spending time with her two beautiful daughters and husband, or walking her dog, Sonya loves ocean sunsets, swimming, and immersing herself in nature. Let her guide you, igniting your inner light and helping you shine brightly, no matter the challenges you face. To learn more about how Sonya can help you, visit her website at www.sonyamcdonald.com.

Caged No More:
Unleashed, Unapologetic, Unshakable

By Sonya McDonald

I used to live in a cage.

Not a physical one. But an emotional, invisible, suffocating kind of cage. The kind you can't see but feel every single day. It looked like smiling through pain. Like saying yes when I meant no. Like putting everyone else's needs ahead of my own until I couldn't even hear the sound of my own voice anymore.

And then my body gave out.

I surrendered.

I gave up the need to control. I was in my thirties when the symptoms first started. Fatigue that no amount of sleep could fix. Pain that moved like a storm through my joints. Brain fog that made me feel like I was watching my life through frosted glass. It was scary. Unrelenting. And confusing. Eventually, I was diagnosed with Rheumatoid Arthritis and Fibromyalgia. And with those two words, my entire identity began to shift.

I didn't just have a disease, I became it.

I went from "Sonya the wife, the nurse, the mom, the woman who could handle anything" to "Sonya, the one who's sick." And once I accepted that identity, I started living like it was true. I pulled back. I isolated. I pretended I was okay on the outside, but I was falling apart on the inside.

Every single day, I lived in fear.

Fear of a flare.

Fear of disappointing others.

Fear that I'd never get my life back.

Fear that I was becoming a burden.

I stopped dreaming. I stopped laughing like I used to. I was alive, but I wasn't really living. I was surviving.

Until one day, I caught a glimpse of my reflection, and I didn't recognize her.

It wasn't the wrinkles or the tired eyes. It was the emptiness. The light in my eyes had gone dim. I was taking care of everyone but myself. And I realized something had to change, because if I didn't change, this disease would consume every part of me.

That's when I signed up for a Tony Robbins event called Unleash the Power Within. Four days. Sixteen hours a day. I didn't know what I was looking for, but I knew I was desperate to find it. And that event cracked me wide open.

Tony said something I'll never forget:

"Your past does not equal your future unless you live there."

That moment was my undoing and my awakening.

I sobbed. I shook. I danced. I screamed into a pillow. I wrote pages and pages of old beliefs I'd been carrying for decades: I'm not enough. I'm too broken. I have to earn love. I'm sick. I'll never be the same.

That weekend, I dug into the parts of myself I'd buried under years of pain, perfectionism, and people-pleasing. I saw all the lies I had been believing, about who I had to be, how I had to perform, how I had to hide my truth to be accepted. That day, I chose something else. I chose me. I surrendered.

And in that moment, I let those beliefs go.

I let go, and I let God.

For the first time in years, I breathed.

That event didn't just change me, it set me free. It made me unleash the woman who had been locked inside the cage of fear for far too long. And I knew I couldn't stop there. I enrolled in a year-long certification program under Tony Robbins and the Robbins-Madanes Training Institute to become a Board Certified Transformational Life Coach.

Because I didn't want to just rise, I wanted to help other women rise, too.

If you're reading this and tears are already falling, I want you to know something.

You're not crazy.

You're not broken.

You're not weak.

You're just tired of being stuck.

You're tired of carrying the weight of everyone's expectations. Tired of being the strong one all the time. Tired of living in fear. Tired of waiting for permission to be the real you.

And that's exactly where your breakthrough begins.

I want you to hear me:

You don't have to live in that cage anymore.

You don't have to live in fear.

You don't have to keep apologizing for who you are.

The moment you decide to set yourself free, you become UNLEASHED.

After that event, everything shifted.

From that moment forward, I started honoring my body. I stopped seeing her as a burden and started seeing her as a messenger. I stopped fighting her and started listening.

I began walking in nature, not to "exercise," but to heal. To breathe. To pray. I drank celery juice. I journaled gratitude. I let the sun touch my skin and remind me I was still alive. Not just surviving. Becoming.

I stopped trying to control everything. I let go of perfectionism. I let go of what others thought. I stopped chasing validation and started listening to my own soul.

That was the true healing.

Because the moment I released control, I finally felt peace. The moment I stopped trying to fix myself, I began to love myself. The moment I stopped being the woman everyone expected, I became the woman I was born to be.

Not perfect. Not polished.

Unshakable. Unapologetic. Free.

And it wasn't just about me anymore.

I knew I had to share this journey. I had to coach women through their own awakening. Women with invisible illnesses. Women with silent anxiety. Women who looked strong on the outside but felt like they were drowning.

As a nurse, I knew the science.

As a woman, I knew the suffering.

As a coach, I now know the way through.

My work became my mission. My pain became my platform. My story became the roadmap for others to find their light, too.

And here's what I know now: You can't heal by hiding. You can't rise by shrinking.

You must be willing to say: "No more cages. No more fear. I choose me."

Here's what most people don't understand: letting go is harder than holding on.

I held on to perfectionism because I thought it kept me safe. If I could control it all—my image, my schedule, my emotions—maybe I wouldn't fall apart. Maybe no one would see how deeply I was already falling.

But that perfectionism? It was a cage, too.

It told me I had to smile when I wanted to cry. It told me I had to serve everyone else before I was allowed to breathe. It told me rest was laziness. That asking for help was weakness. That slowing down meant I was failing.

It lied.

Letting go of perfectionism felt like jumping off a cliff without a parachute. But what I found was, I didn't fall. I flew.

I started saying no. Without guilt. Without explaining myself.

I started saying yes. To rest. To joy. To the slow mornings with my girls and enjoying a walk in the sunset. To things that didn't look "productive," but felt deeply nourishing.

I released the need to be everything to everyone. I stopped performing for approval.

I even stopped trying to heal "perfectly." I gave myself permission to have bad days, flare-up days, doubt days, and love myself through them all.

Because healing isn't linear. It's messy and sacred.

Some days, I needed movement. Some days, I needed stillness.

Some days, I soared. Others, I simply survived. And that was enough.

And in that softness, I found strength.

I became the woman I was looking for in my hardest seasons.

Not the one who had it all figured out.

But the one who could sit in the dark and still remember her light.

I stopped asking, "When will I feel normal again?" and started asking, "How can I feel like me again?"

And here's the truth: the old me wasn't coming back. She was never meant to.

She broke for a reason, so I could rise.

I started building a new version of me. One rooted in grace.

One who didn't hustle for her worth.

One who chose alignment over approval.

One who knew that boundaries weren't walls; they were bridges to freedom.

I looked at my daughters and realized: I'm not just healing for me, I'm healing for them, too.

So they never feel they have to be perfect to be loved.

So they never think their illness or pain disqualifies them from joy.

So they know their worth is non-negotiable.

They watched me fall. Now, I let them watch me rise.

They hear me say, "Mom needs rest today," and they know rest is sacred.

They see me walk in the morning light, and they know movement is medicine.

They watch me coach and write and speak, and they see that purpose can grow from pain.

They are learning to live unleashed, because I chose to.

She laughs louder now.

She rests unapologetically.

She sets boundaries that protect her peace like her life depends on it, because it does.

She wakes up every day and thanks God that she gets another chance to live out her purpose.

She's not perfect. She's present.

She's not fearless. She's courageous.

She's not cured. She's committed to herself, her calling, and her healing.

I don't wait for permission anymore.

I don't wait for the right time.

I don't shrink to make people comfortable.

And I don't confuse being kind with being silent.

I speak. I shine. I serve. I stand tall.

Because there are women watching.

My daughters.

Strangers who see me and think, "If she did it, maybe I can, too."

I carry them with me into every room I enter.

Every coaching session.

Every talk.

Every page I write.

I'm not just a survivor; I'm a guide. A mirror. A voice reminding other women: You are not your diagnosis. You are not your fear. You are not your failures. You are not too late.

You are not broken.

You are buried under fear, shame, and years of performing.

But the real you? She's still in there.

And she's waiting.

Not for everything to be perfect.

Not for someone else to save her.

But for you to choose her.

I'm here to tell you it's safe to choose her now.

It's safe to stop running.

It's safe to take off the mask.

It's safe to stop performing and start becoming.

Your healing doesn't have to look like mine.

But your wholeness?

It starts the same way, by deciding to stop living in a story that was never yours.

You get to rewrite it now.

You get to rise now.

Because cages are comfortable until they start choking you.

And maybe today is the day you stop being comfortable and start being courageous.

Maybe today is the day you say:

"I want to live unleashed."

But here's the truth that set me free.

I stopped trying to be the version of me that didn't exist anymore.

I let her go.

The one who smiled through pain to make others comfortable.

The one who performed to be accepted.

The one who shrank to keep the peace.

I buried her with grace and thanked her for getting me this far.

But she couldn't come with me here. Not to this part of the story.

Because the woman I am now?

She knows that tears are sacred.

That strength looks like asking for help.

That beauty lives in the brave.

I used to think that surrender was a sign of weakness.

Now, I know it's holy.

It's not about giving up, it's about giving it over.

To God.

To healing.

To peace.

I no longer beg for love, I rest in it.

I no longer fight for visibility; I stand in my light.

Letting go of control didn't break me. It built me.

When I surrendered the outcome, God showed me a new way.

He whispered, "You don't have to carry this anymore."

And for the first time, I believed Him.

I stopped trying to be less.

Less emotional.

Less sensitive.

Less "high maintenance."

I stopped apologizing for needing rest.

For being intuitive.

For being different.

Now, I honor the quiet wisdom of my soul.

I honor the soft strength in my voice.

I honor the sacred fire in my purpose.

And I honor the woman who chose herself, even when it was terrifying.

Because becoming unleashed wasn't about becoming someone new.

It was about coming home.

And now I know this:

I was never broken. I was buried. And this was my rising.

You're here because something inside you knows it's time.

Time to rise.

Time to take back your life.

Time to stop shrinking and start shining.

If you're ready to step into the woman you were created to be, fully, boldly, and unapologetically, then I want to walk beside you.

As a transformational life coach, a registered nurse with over 30 years of experience, an author, and speaker, I help women just like you ignite their light and transform their lives.

I've lived it.

I've walked through it.

And now I coach women who are ready to stop living in survival mode and start thriving.

Whether you're struggling with burnout, invisible illness, perfectionism, fear, or just the deep sense that you were made for more, I'm here to remind you: You don't have to do it alone.

Let's turn your pain into purpose.

Let's rewrite your story.

Let's unleash the woman inside you who is tired of pretending she's okay.

You were never too much.

You were never too late.

And you are not broken, you are becoming.

If you're ready to rise, visit me at www.sonyamcdonald.com and let's ignite your light together.

Because you're not just meant to survive, you're meant to shine.

And girl,

You were never meant to live caged. You were born to be unshakable.

I know what it feels like to break. To scream into the silence. To wonder if the light will ever return.

But here's what I also know:

Your breakdown is not the end. It's the beginning of your breakthrough.

I didn't write this chapter just to tell my story. I wrote it to hand you the key to your own cage.

If something inside you is stirring right now, pay attention. That's your soul remembering who she is.

Don't go back to sleep.

This is your moment.

The girl inside you is ready to rise. Not someday, now.

Because the story doesn't end here.

In fact, this is just the beginning.

In my solo book, *Unshakable*, coming out this summer, I tell the whole truth about the journey that took me from surviving to soaring. It's more than a book. It's a movement. A blueprint. A light in the dark.

And if this chapter lit something in you, wait until you turn that first page.

Because you, my sister, are not just meant to survive.

You're meant to rise. To roar. And to become… Unshakable.

Journal Prompt:
What belief do you need to release today so you can finally live free?

Karen Rudolf

Founder of Tranquil SOULutions

https://www.linkedin.com/in/tranquilsoulutions/
https://www.facebook.com/karen.rudolf.14/
https://www.instagram.com/karenrudolf_/
www.TranquilSOULutions.com

Karen Rudolf is a transformative Life Strategist, "Catalyst for Change," and 9 X International collaborative Best-Selling Author. She is the founder of Tranquil SOULutions and the developer of the 'Tranquil SOULutions Clarity Tool,' which is a Mindset Mirror for shifting perception. She is dedicated to empowering personal and professional growth through a "W"holistic approach. With a background in nursing and extensive training in the 7 Pillars of Health, she empowers individuals to overcome challenges and thrive through effective communication, self-leadership, boosting self-esteem, and fostering "W"holistic well-being. She also decreases stress, resulting in a "W"holistic approach to personal and professional growth. Her work shifts perceptions and nurtures resilience and peace, making her a trusted guide in life's journey.

Unleashing Me:
From Silenced to Soulfully Empowered

By Karen Rudolf

There was a moment when everything changed. Not in the way a lightning bolt strikes or the ground shakes—but in a quiet, powerful inner declaration.

I was standing over my mother, who lay on the floor, surrounded by 19 medications. A lifetime of masking symptoms had finally caught up to her. And I realized something that would shift the course of my life forever:

"The buck stops here."

That moment awakened something fierce and focused inside me. After growing up in a world where children were meant to be seen, not heard—and then entering a profession where nurses were to be quiet observers rather than questioners—I had had enough. I had asked a simple question about whether we were truly *treating* patients or just *managing* them. The answer I received was silence, dismissal, and more scripts and pills.

But I couldn't ignore the truth anymore. I felt it deep down in my core.

I decided then and there to become a **catalyst for change.**

The Cost of People-Pleasing

As far back as I can remember, I played the role of the good girl. The one who said yes. The one who smiled even when her heart was breaking. I believed that to be loved, I had to earn it by overgiving and under-asking. The more I tried to be enough, the more invisible I felt.

The result? Disappointment after disappointment. A growing inner voice that whispered I wasn't smart enough, worthy enough, or strong enough, and that I *must be stupid*.

I shrank. I played small. I got taken advantage of on so many levels and ... I lost *myself*.

The Moment I Found My Voice

Years later, during the emotional storm of my divorce, a new moment of reckoning arrived.

My paralegal, Cliff, looked me dead in the eye and said:

"If you don't find your voice and stop being the victim, you'll lose your children."

That hit me like a tidal wave.

I was their mother—their first teacher, their first mentor. What was I teaching them? That silence and suffering were survival skills? That staying small was safe? That question had me ask myself what else in my life I was losing besides exuberant amounts of money in attorney fees and a lot of time fretting and worrying over things I had no control over, rather than focusing on what's at hand.

No more.

That day, I made another vow: No one was going to take my children from me, and that old way of being had to die so a new version of me could rise.

The Inner Journey Begins

It seemed to me that we were all here to expand. I began looking outside of myself. Before I came to realize it had been within me all along.

I delved into personal development: books, tapes, courses, coaching, and spiritual teachings. But it wasn't about gathering knowledge—it was about reclaiming myself.

I stopped blaming others. I stopped pointing fingers outward. And I started taking radical responsibility.

I let go of old judgments. I chose forgiveness. And most importantly, I chose *myself*! I began to *listen*—to my body, to my heart, to my truth.

Each course, each coaching session aligned with my greater calling: to be a catalyst for change in a "W"-holistic way—addressing not just symptoms, but the whole being: mental, emotional, physical, and spiritual.

That's when I decided to put a "W" in front of the word "holistic"—because we are WHOLE humans. Whole, complete, and worthy right now.

Back in the day, I couldn't make a decision to save my life. It felt like I'd take one step forward and two steps back. I'd stick my neck out of my comfort zone only to retreat back to my safe space. This definitely kept me from moving forward. The journey was a slow one.

I was doing my usual six hours of carpooling back then, and when I completed my audiobook, I reached out to my daughter to ask her if she had one. After looking over her huge list, one book that really stood out to me was Shonda Rhimes' *The Year of Yes*. Not knowing a thing about it, I decided to listen and listen I did!

I decided to be a "Yes" to my own life as well!! It was challenging, exciting, exuberant, and quite the stretch to say the least. Was it easy? *Heck NO!* I was committed to myself. A path of transformation isn't for everyone. It doesn't come with ease, it's not always comfortable, and it's certainly not predictable. There are no guarantees—only the promise that if you keep showing up, keep leaning in, and keep trusting the process, you will emerge stronger, clearer, and more connected than ever before.

It means stepping into the unknown. It means embracing the unfamiliar, even when everything in you craves certainty. It means feeling, deep in your soul, a pull and a knowing that you weren't meant to stay where you are. It requires the courage to honor that call and embrace the uncertainty of who you are becoming.

Becoming Sassy, Classy, and Badassy

I began embracing my **sassy confidence**—something that felt completely foreign to my shy, reserved self. But I kept showing up, feeling the fear, and doing it anyway.

And guess what? Nobody made me wrong. I wasn't judged or ridiculed. I was becoming free. It felt invigorating, exciting in some ways, and I looked forward to showing up.

That gave me the courage to step into **classy confidence**—the grace of being raw and real with myself, and then sharing that authenticity with others.

As I learned new tools and deepened my emotional resilience, I saw how much of the pain we carry begins inside. And I knew my mission wasn't just to support others in feeling better—it was to support them to **heal** from the inside out.

Tools for the Journey

I created a method called **The Butterfly Technique**—a reminder to pause, change the narrative, and shift the energy of the moment. Just like a butterfly that must transform in the cocoon, we, too, must allow ourselves the space to *become more than we know ourselves to be*.

It took courage to change, and I hadn't waited for permission to grow. And then came my badassy, bold action era. The version of me that no longer waited for others' thoughts, feelings, or opinions unless I sought them with intention. I moved forward with more confidence, clarity, purpose, and a full heart.

After more than 15 years of trial and error, growth and expansion, I created the **Tranquil SOULutions Clarity Tool**™—a digital offering designed to support others in doing what I've done: tapping into their inner compass and *trusting* it.

This tool is a culmination of my journey—a guided way to access your inner truth, to activate healing and clarity, and to live from a place of peace and power.

To the Woman Still Finding Her Way

If you're reading this and you feel stuck—please know you're not alone.

I see you.

I was you.

The past holds clues, yes—but it *doesn't* hold your power.

Your power lies in the choices you make right now.
To forgive. To shift. To rise. To rewrite your story.

You are the **architect** of your life.
You get to design it with fun, flair, and fierce love for your future.

So unleash your sassy confidence.
Embrace your classy grace.
And take bold, badassy action.

Join the ripple.
Share your story.
Rise together with us.

Because the next chapter? It begins *now*.
And it begins *with you*. Your story matters, your life matters, and perhaps your story will make a difference in another's life.

Unleashing Her: A Final Reflection

As I reflect on the woman I've become—the one who now walks boldly with clarity, courage, and deep compassion—I see the ripple I've created not just in my own life, but in the lives of others. Through every story I've written, every client I've served, and every truth I've dared to speak, I've embodied what it means to *unleash her*.

It's not about being fearless. It's about feeling the fear and rising anyway.

It's about claiming your story—not just the polished parts, but the messy, raw, transformative moments that shape you.

And it's about choosing every single day to trust your voice, your vision, and your value. Remind yourself daily: YOU ARE WORTH IT! You Matter!

The **Tranquil SOULutions Clarity Tool™** is a byproduct of that trust. It is a living resource designed for women who are ready to rise, break boundaries, and embrace the next chapter of their lives with intention. It is the tool I created so others could stop searching outside themselves and start listening within.

Because when a woman reclaims her clarity, she doesn't just rewrite her own story—she lights the way for others to do the same.

So, to every woman reading this: Your soul already knows the way. All that's left is for you to listen.

Unleash her. Unleash *you*. The next chapter begins now. The clarity lives within you!

Lovely LaGuerre

Founder and CEO of Pure Heavenly Hair, LLC

https://www.twitter.com/Heavenly_Pure
https://www.facebook.com/pureheavenlyhairboutique
https://pureheavenlyhair.com/
https://instagram.com/pureheavenlyhair
1.Pure Heavenly Hair and Beauty
https://pureheavenlyhair.com/
2.Commercial and Luxury Real Estate
https://lovelysellsvegas.com/

ABOUT PURE HEAVENLY HAIR & BEAUTY

At Pure Heavenly Hair and Beauty our commitment to inclusivity and individuality is at the heart of everything we do. We celebrate all forms of beauty backgrounds, understanding that each person's journey is unique. Whether it's through our deeply moisturizing lip oils that enhance your natural glow or our go to wigs hair collections that bring life back to your locks, Pure Heavenly is here to honor and elevate your essence in every way. What truly makes us different is our belief in the power of connections with others. When you choose Pure Heavenly Hair and Beauty, you're choosing more than just a brand. You're embracing a lifestyle of conscious beauty, where every product is a ritual, every application a moment of self-care, and every result a testament to the heavenly within you. Come Unleash Your Beauty From Within!Join us in our mission to redefine your beauty purely, naturally, and beautifully. Experience the heavenly touch of our products and discover what it means to truly elevate your essence with Pure Heavenly Hair and Beauty!Pure Beauty | Pure Confidence | Purely Heavenly You!

The Bold, Beautiful Rise of My Entrepreneurial Journey

By Lovely LaGuerre

They say every woman holds a fire inside her, a spark that's just waiting for the right moment, the right reason, or the right rebellion to ignite. For me, that fire started as a whisper. A quiet, persistent tug at my soul that said, "You're made for more." Not more in the sense of material things, but more impact, more freedom, more purpose.

I am Lovely LaGuerre, and this is my unapologetically bold story.

I didn't start with a silver spoon. I didn't have a trust fund, a blueprint, or a lineup of mentors cheering me on. What I had was a vision and a heart that refused to settle. I had seen too many brilliant women, gifted, driven, dim their light because the world told them their dreams were "too much." Too risky. Too out there. Too loud.

But I wasn't interested in shrinking to fit a mold I didn't design.

My journey into entrepreneurship wasn't one lightning bolt of inspiration. It was a series of tiny revolutions, late-night ideas scribbled in notebooks, tear-streaked prayers whispered after failure, and the electric thrill of saying "yes" when fear screamed "no." Every risk I took was a message to myself: You're allowed to trust your instincts. You're allowed to be powerful.

Confidence Is a Muscle, Not a Gift

Confidence didn't come wrapped in a bow. I had to build it, flex it, and keep pushing forward. Early on, I learned that no one was coming to grant me permission. I had to take it. I had to believe that my ideas were worth something even when no one else saw the value yet.

There were moments when I questioned everything. When the bank account looked more like a joke than a business asset. When launches failed. When clients ghosted. When imposter syndrome set up camp in my head like an uninvited roommate. But each time, I got back up stronger, wiser, louder.

Because that's what women do. We rise. Again and again.

Fear Is a Compass, Not a Stop Sign

One of the greatest lessons I've learned is that fear isn't a red light; it's a GPS. If something scares me, it usually means I'm going in the right direction of growth. I started chasing those fears like breadcrumbs to my future.

I took risks others warned me against. I walked away from comfort. I launched bold ideas that felt like leaping off cliffs without a parachute. And every time I landed not perfectly, but purposefully, I built wings on the way down.

What I found was this: The life I was meant to live was on the other side of every fear I faced.

Unleashing Her

Somewhere along the way, I realized this wasn't just about me. My story wasn't just mine to keep; it was a blueprint, a mirror, a rallying cry.

Unleashing her became more than a personal mantra. It turned into a movement. A pulse. A permission slip for every woman who's ever been told she's "too much" or "not enough."

To unleash her is to trust her.

To unleash her is to break every invisible boundary.

To unleash her is to rise, roar, and reclaim everything that once felt out of reach.

It's time for women to stop waiting for the right moment, become the moment, and be the moment. To stop apologizing for their brilliance, their ambition, their fire.

You Don't Need to Be Ready, You Need to Be Brave

If I had waited until I was ready, I'd still be waiting. There's no perfect moment. There's no magical level of experience where doubt disappears and clarity rings like a bell. Starting ugly, starting scared, starting uncertain, that's how greatness begins.

I've learned that bravery is a decision, not a personality trait. And the more we act in courage, the more it multiplies.

I built my brand one late night, one brave post, one bold decision at a time. I poured my heart into every product, every service, every message. I made my business a reflection of my values: authenticity, empowerment, and transformation.

And I made space for other women to do the same.

The Ripple Effect

When one woman rises, she lifts others. That's the beauty of this journey. We're not in competition, we're in collaboration. Every time I stepped out of my comfort zone, I saw other women do the same. Every time I shared my truth, another woman found the courage to speak hers.

Unleashing her doesn't stop at one woman. It creates a ripple. A revolution. A legacy.

The woman I am today? She's not the same woman who started this journey.

She's louder. Not in volume but in truth. She's not waiting to be chosen anymore. She built her table, set the seats, and made space for other women to sit beside her, not beneath her.

And let me tell you: building that woman wasn't easy. It was gritty. It was messy. It was deeply personal.

I had to unlearn so many things. Like the belief that struggle equals failure. Being multi-passionate meant I lacked focus. That asking for help was a weakness. That I needed to be ten steps ahead to be worthy of success.

Wrong. All of it.

The truth? Every version of me, tired, thriving, messy, and magnetic, was worthy. Right where she was. Right as she was. That's the gift of entrepreneurship; it's not just about building a business, it's about building you.

Your Vision Is Valid, Even if They Don't Get It Yet

People will question your vision. Sometimes, it will be the ones closest to you. Not because they don't love you, but because they can't see what you see. They haven't caught the fire that's burning inside you.

I had to get comfortable being misunderstood. I had to learn that I wasn't building for applause, I was building for alignment. And once I stopped trying to explain myself to people who weren't aligned with my mission, everything shifted.

Doors opened. Resources came. The right tribe found me. Because when you stop shrinking, you make space for a real connection.

Pivoting with Power

I've rebranded. Relaunched. Reimagined my business more times than I can count. And every pivot was proof that I wasn't afraid to evolve.

If there's anything entrepreneurship teaches you, it's that change isn't the enemy; it will be your power to move.

The key is to stay grounded in your why, but flexible in your how.

Sometimes, the ideas I was obsessed with didn't work. And that's okay. I didn't fail. I learned. I adjusted. I moved forward with sharper vision.

Rest Is Strategy | Not Surrender

There were seasons when I worked 14-hour days, where hustle culture had me believing I needed to be doing everything, all the time. But burnout doesn't build empires. Alignment does.

I started permitting myself to pause. To protect my peace. To rest, not quit.

That shift in mindset was a game-changer. I began building from overflow instead of depletion. And my business started reflecting that clarity, creativity, and impact.

Unleash Her: The Movement

This is where Unleash Her turned into something bigger than me.

I saw the women around me, the ones starting side hustles after bedtime stories, the ones building brands in the cracks of their 9-to-5, the ones dreaming big in silence because they feared judgment, and I knew they needed a space.

A space to be seen. To be celebrated. To be reminded that they don't have to do this alone.

Unleash Her became that space. A movement. A moment. A manifesto.

It says: You are not too much. You are not behind. You are not alone.

It's a call to lock arms for every woman who's ever played small out of fear. It's a bold invitation to break free, take up space, and lead with legacy.

Because when we unleash her, we change the game.

Legacy Over Likes

There's a lot of noise out here. Social media likes. Vanity metrics. Highlight reels.

But impact? That's deeper. It's the DM from a stranger saying, "Your story gave me the courage to start." It's the mentee who says, "You showed me what's possible." It's the daughter who says, "Mom, you're my hero."

That's legacy.

I stopped chasing quick wins and started building something timeless. I want my brand to outlive trends. I want my story to echo long after I'm gone. Not because it was perfect, but because it was real.

Empowered Women Empower Women

I'm a firm believer that empowered women aren't gatekeepers. We share. We mentor. We pass the mic and hold the door open.

That's why I now strategize with other women in business. Why I pour into women to dream bigger.

Because we're not just building businesses, we're building futures.

Unleash Her Is a Revolution

It's not a hashtag. It's a heartbeat.

It's every woman who's ever dared to rise, even when the odds were stacked.

It's the ones who said yes to the risk.

Yes to the growth.

Yes to the fire.

And now? We rise together.

We amplify each other's voices.

We invest in each other's visions.

We rewrite the rules and flip the script.

Because Unleash Her isn't just a moment. It's a movement.

Building Beyond Limits, Leading with Legacy

As I look back, I don't just see milestones, I see moments. Moments where I could've backed down... but didn't. Moments where I could've stayed silent... but spoke. Moments where I could've waited for permission... but chose to lead.

Because that's what this journey has taught me: True success isn't about the destination, it's about who you become on the way there.

It's the woman I became when I said yes to the unknown.

It's the fire I lit when I took my dreams off the shelf.

It's the tribe I found when I dared to rise.

I didn't get here by being fearless; I got here by moving through the fear. By trusting my voice, even when it shook me to the core. By choosing growth over comfort, and vision over validation.

And now? I stand not just as a businesswoman but as a builder of legacies.

You Are the Blueprint

For a long time, I searched for templates. Strategies. Step-by-step guides.

But eventually, I realized something powerful: I am the blueprint.

My story.

My voice.

My values.

My path.

No one else can do it like me. And no one else can do it like you either.

That's what makes you powerful. Your journey isn't a detour; it's the design. Everything you've walked through, everything you've overcome, it was never random. It was refining you. Preparing you. Positioning you.

You don't have to fit into someone else's mold. You're allowed to build your lane and set it on fire.

The World Needs What You Carry

If there's one thing I want women everywhere to know, it's this: Your voice matters. Your dream matters. Your story is needed.

You don't have to wait until you have it all figured out. Start with what you have. Where you are. As you are.

Because there's someone out there who needs your version of the dream. Your perspective. Your magic.

And when you unleash the woman you were born to be, you permit other women to do the same.

The Call To Rise

Unleash Her isn't about perfection. It's about power.

It's not about being fearless. It's about being faithful to the call, to the dream, to the woman within.

It's not just about creating wealth; it's about creating waves.

Unleash Her is a movement for the bold, the brave, and the becoming.

It's for the woman building her empire while healing from heartbreak.

It's for the woman launching her brand while she is still creating.

It's for the woman showing up for herself for the first time in a long time.

It's for the woman who dares to say:

"I am not what happened to me. I am what I choose to become."

We Are the Legacy

The truth is, we're writing history. Every step we take, every boundary we break, every glass ceiling we shatter, it matters.

Because when we rise, generations rise with us.

That's what gets me out of bed in the morning. Not just the profits. Not the likes. But the purpose. The ripple effect. The legacy we're building every single day.

And now I stand here, not just as a woman who dreamed but as a woman who did.

A woman who dared to Unleash Her.

To Every Woman Reading This

This is your invitation.

To stop playing small.

To silence the doubt.

To trust your voice.

To leap.

To pivot boldly.

To launch loudly.

To show up for your dreams like they're already yours.

Because they are.

You are not behind.

You are not too late.

You are not too much.

You are exactly what this world needs right now.

And when you rise, you remind another woman that she can, too.

Kaila

Author

https://www.facebook.com/profile.php?id=61564802221645
https://www.instagram.com/kailanike.author/
https://www.tiktok.com/@kailanikeauthor
https://kailanike.com/

Born and raised in British Columbia, Kaila Nike is a dedicated mother raising two wonderful sons. While she earned a diploma in social work, writing has always been her true passion. Finding solace and expression in her words, Kaila focuses on crafting engaging narratives through poetry and romantasy.

Unapologetic

By Kaila

Fitting Inside the Box

"You should never dye your hair blonde." The words from my eighth-grade crush held more meaning than anything else in those days. His opinion mattered. This wasn't the beginning or the end of allowing someone else's opinions to dictate my actions and/or behaviour. From a young age, I, like many others, was programmed to adhere to the desires of others. It's the way we grew up. The problem with that, though, is that I was being kept in a box. A box that was built to please others and completely disregard my own feelings and individuality. He didn't know that, though, and at the time, neither did I.

However it happened, pleasing other people somehow became a strong foundation of my internal belief system. I was raised by my parents, yes. But I was also raised by my grandparents, friends, teachers, aunts, uncles, cousins, community members, acquaintances, and even television. From the day we are born, our belief systems are shaped by the people and the environment around us.

One thing that I had eventually learned is that the same message was being broadcast all across the board, and most of us aren't even consciously aware of it until much later in our more mature years. We're constantly being told how to behave, how to fit in, and what others expect of us. And to some extent, it's not a bad thing. We want to fit into society and create meaningful connections. But it can also be harmful if it's taken too far. And for a majority of my life, that was the case. It didn't just begin or end with "never dye your hair blonde"; it's so much deeper than that. Boundaries were crossed, and I was programmed to accept it. It took me years before I understood this. And all the while, it was hurting me and didn't allow me to become who I truly was, deep within. My growth was stunted.

I grew up to be a people pleaser. There are many things that have contributed to this side of my personality. I was always concerned whether I'm accepted, if I hurt someone's feelings, if I didn't act or behave a certain way, that no one would like me, to pacify an abuser, to avoid conflict, I was insecure and had low self-esteem. And if I said the wrong thing to someone, I would dwell on it for hours about how that could have gone so differently. I was really hard on myself; there was little to no self-compassion. But what was the most hurtful, though, was when someone had wronged me. Over the years, I had learned to accept it, let it roll off my shoulders, or forget about it; otherwise, I'd be the one who isn't accepted into society. I carried a lot of secrets that were filled with pain for a very long time, for the sake of fitting in, pleasing others, fear of rejection, embarrassment, and the list goes on. I got really good at fitting in, I learned how to dress, how to talk, and even how to keep secrets. Secrets that hurt me. Secrets that I would carry forever, all for the sake of sparing someone else's feelings over my own.

If this isn't your experience, then that's great! And I am truly happy for you. However, for many of us, it really is our reality. So, how do we overcome it, how do we break out of this metaphorical prison that we're trapped in? How do we live for ourselves and not for others? How do we begin to feel comfortable in our own skin and with our own thoughts, without caring so much about what other people think of us, and start having more respect for our own thoughts and feelings?

Climbing Out of the Box

Well, the answer isn't as simple as it seems, and of course, it's always easier said than done. If we want to be true to ourselves and live for ourselves, then I have good news for you! There are actionable steps that we can take. It will be work, though, and it might not be easy. But it's worth a try, isn't it? To feel what it's like to live for ourselves, to place our own happiness and well-being above others, is a pretty incredible way to live. Is it selfish? Heck yes! And that's perfectly okay! Own it.

When we shift from being a people pleaser to a self-pleaser, it's going to feel really uncomfortable, and it's going to take a lot of practice. It definitely won't happen overnight; there are skills that need to be learned and implemented. Think about it: You spent your whole life serving other people, and now suddenly you're going to shift that energy onto yourself. Your whole perspective will need to shift. And trust me, it's not easy. I was raised to be a people pleaser, and it took me years of personal development, skill building, and self-love to finally figure out how to put myself first, to live for me, so that I can create the dream life that I want for myself. A life that isn't being ruled by other people's wants or opinions. If you want to learn some actionable steps on how to take your life back and own it, then read on! This list is not exhaustive, but it's definitely a good place to start.

Own it, Boss!

1. No. The power of no. Say it out loud, shout it, whisper it, say it in your head, repeat it over and over again until it feels natural. At first, it's going to feel uncomfortable. Especially when you say *no* to someone else for the first time. However, it's an incredibly powerful word. Keep in mind that when you do say no, you don't owe anyone an explanation to go with it. When you have the courage to say no, it sets clear boundaries while prioritizing and empowering yourself. If saying yes doesn't align with your own wants, needs, or goals, then why say yes to it?

I could go on and on about the importance of this small and significant word, but that's not what this chapter is about. There are many books about having the courage to say *no*. I highly recommend *How to Say NO Without Feeling Guilty* by Patti Breitman and Connie Hatch. Now, take a deep breath. You got this.

2. Set boundaries. This goes hand in hand with learning how to say no. Boundaries are so incredibly important to protect ourselves, our time, and our sanity. Communication comes into play here as well. It's important to communicate those boundaries to others, no matter how uncomfortable it may seem at first. *Set Boundaries, Find Peace* by Nedra Glover Tawwab is a great place to start when learning how to set boundaries, whether you are a people pleaser or someone who just needs to build strength and confidence, along with some new skills. It's time to put you first, girl.

3. Self-awareness. The more self-aware you are of yourself, the easier it is to make decisions and live for yourself. If you are unable to figure out who you are, someone else will decide it for you. Be true to yourself. What do you love to do? What are you passionate about? Who are your favourite people/artists/public figures, etc.? What are your hobbies? How do you like to spend your spare time? Do you like to read, binge-watch shows, play sports, dress up and go out, paint, and go hiking? The list goes on. The more you know about yourself, the more confident you'll become, the stronger your connections with others can be, the easier it will be to put yourself first, and so on. If you're putting your needs and desires first, you will find yourself in a community of like-minded individuals who are more accepting of who you are. For example, I love to read and am a part of an online community of like-minded people who also love to read the same types of books that I do. It's something we all have in common, and it is a positive environment. A place of belonging.

If you're not quite sure what makes you, you, then I suggest some research. Prioritize your needs over the needs of others. Try some new things and step out of your comfort zone a little bit. The more that you love to do, the more you will become in tune with yourself, making it easier to be true to yourself. If you try something and you don't like it, don't do it. This is a long game, so be patient with yourself. Especially if you've been told what to do and what to like (the media is good at that), then it may seem unnatural to start exploring different and unusual things. But once you find out more about who you are and what makes you, you, then you're gonna be so much happier. I'm sure of it. Not only that, but the more self-aware you are, the easier it will be to say no. For more on self-awareness, I recommend *The Art of Self-Awareness: To Conquer Your Life You Must Know Who You Are* by Alejandra Llamas.

4. Seek support. There are millions of people in the world who can likely relate to what you're going through. Seeking support is not a weakness; it's a strength. Vulnerability is a strength. No one has to go through anything alone. There are many different avenues a person can take when seeking support or advice. What works for one might not work for all, but listed here are some ideas to get the brainstorming started. Counselling and therapy are the first things that come to mind, of course. Friends and family can also be an option; perhaps there is someone close to you whom you can confide in. Support groups, this could be online or in person, depending on where you live. Different cities will have different supports in place. There are plenty of online support groups. If you're unable to find one that suits your specific needs, create one. Chances are that if you're feeling a certain way or dealing with certain issues, then it's likely that others are as well. Self-help books/workshops are also a great resource, and if you're an introvert or a private person, you don't need to confide in others if you're relying on books. However, I must say that as someone who is introverted, seeking support from others that I trust has made a world of a difference for me.

5. Compassion. Remember that we are only human. We are not perfect, and we never will be. It's okay to have compassion and understanding with yourself. We all go through different experiences that shape us into who we are. It's okay to strive to be better. It's also okay to have some flaws. That's what makes us human, embrace it. Become friends with the things that make us perfectly imperfect. It's how we will learn to grow and eventually thrive. Although there will always be something, it seems, that we have to work on, you're here, and you're trying. And that alone is significant. Congratulate yourself. As cliché as it sounds, give yourself that pat on your back. You deserve it. Even better, let me extend an air-hug to you!

In Summary

We've been over five steps on how to unleash our inner power, but you must have some questions. Like, I'm a mom, a wife, a sibling, a daughter, a friend, I have responsibilities, a duty to others. While in a sense that's true, it doesn't have to be your entire identity. I am a mom, too—a single mom at that—and my responsibility is to my children. But that doesn't mean I can't take some much-needed time to myself. And truth be told, others will respect you for taking care of yourself first. They will see it, learn from it, and adopt it. We teach others how to treat us. It's our duty to teach those around us how others should treat them, as well. My days consist of waking up, getting the kids ready for the day, feeding them, cleaning the house, driving them around, etc., yes, those are my duties as their parent. BUT I don't hesitate to take an hour each night to have a nice hot bath while I read a book or watch the latest show. That's my time, and they know that and respect it. One of my biggest outlets, believe it or not, is either reading or video games. I spend all day, every day, caring for my loved ones, and that's a duty that I cherish. I wouldn't have it any other way. But some days I need to just relax, and my way of doing that is to put on a headset and play video games.

It's all about balance. If you're feeling stressed or overwhelmed, your body is trying to communicate with you. It means something is up, and it's probably that you're not putting your own needs first. Listen to your instincts. Our instincts are an incredible God-given gift that shouldn't be taken for granted. Those around you will love and respect you for putting yourself first. And better yet, you're teaching them how to put themselves first as well. And those who don't? Well, that's on them. They clearly have baggage they need to work on.

If I had allowed myself to continue to be a people pleaser and live for others, then I never would have found my own way. I never would have begun writing, let alone for the world to see, leaving it open for the world to critique my work. Like I said, there is strength in vulnerability. If you'd like to check out my debut novel, *Mystique*, scan the QR code below. This is just an example of what it can look like when you fight through the fear and begin to live for yourself.

So do the thing you want to do, say *no* to the night out that you're dreading going to, do that activity that you actually want to do, seek support in those you trust, communicate your needs, respect yourself, and lastly, dye your hair the freaking colour you want! Unleash that powerful woman within. Allow your next chapter to begin with newfound confidence. And most of all, be unapologetically you!

Mystique is a "romantasy" novel about a single mother raising two boys, who falls head over heels for a mysterious and charming cowboy. Unbeknownst to her, this man has a dark side that threatens to destroy everything she's created.

Erica Elliott

WarriorHeart Healing Hearts, LLC
Speaker, Author, Counselor, Brain Health Coach, and Consultant

https://www.linkedin.com/in/erica-elliott-ms-lpc-b90911150
https://www.facebook.com/warriorheartxo
https://www.instagram.com/warriorheartxo
https://msha.ke/warriorheartxo

I possess a Master's Degree in Counseling Psychology and have invested over three decades in my career as a Licensed Counselor, Certified Brain Health Coach, and Certified Health Integrative Medicine Professional. My expertise encompasses a broad spectrum of therapeutic approaches, such as Neurobiology, ADHD and Neurodiversity, Somatic Therapy, Energy Medicine, NLP, CBT, RET, EFT, TFT, Theology, EMDR, the Gottman Method, alongside Mindfulness and Meditation. I am an international acclaimed author, speaker and spent over a decade in the military. I am the owner of WarriorHeart Healing Hearts where I champion a comprehensive healing philosophy that harmonizes the mind, body, and spirit. I help individuals clear up the mess to discover their MASTERPIECE using a combination of healing modalities to rapidly rewire for success!

A Journey to Clarity and Freedom

By Erica Elliott

It wasn't your typical day. It was actually what I would call a magical day, but not because things were going great. In fact, it was quite the opposite.

It had been nearly two years since I had COVID, and I was still working through a lot—mentally, emotionally, physically. Brain fog, anxiety, panic attacks, myalgia, heart issues, fatigue that just wouldn't go away, no matter how much I slept or rested. I had started doing hyperbaric oxygen treatments to help so much. They helped me feel more like myself again, at least enough to start thinking a bit more about how to live more with acceptance and adapting to my new norm. But something inside me still felt stuck and lost. I knew I needed something more...something life-giving. A spark. A shift. Really just to get out of the four walls.

And that's when I picked up the phone.

As a counselor for over 30 years and a brain health coach who has seen the full spectrum of human emotion and experience, I've helped thousands of people through grief, trauma, anxiety, burnout, and more. I've studied the science, Bible scriptures, natural pathic medicines, and lots of healing modalities—but the truth is, when it hits, your healing doesn't only happen in therapy rooms. Healing happens in life. In exploration. In laughter. In relationships.

That day, I felt a prompting in my spirit to call my daughter.

She was seven months pregnant, her husband was deployed overseas, and I could hear the exhaustion in her voice when she picked up. I said, "Hey, sweetie, I miss you. I know we've both been between these four walls way too much. What if we made a little plan to go out once a week—do something fun and explore some new places? Like mini vacations. And who knows...maybe we could film it and help others get out of their own ruts, too. I know sitting behind four walls isn't good for us."

There was a pause. Then, she seemed interested and excited. "That actually sounds kind of good, and I can film my content clothing while we are out. I do miss getting out more, and that sounds fun." I will say she was a bit uneasy about trying some foods herself but was willing to at least get out of the house.

I didn't know it at the time, but that one phone call would completely shift the course of both of our lives.

Let me back up a bit and share why this mattered so much.

My daughter and I have always been close—truly connected. She's my miracle baby, I almost lost her in pregnancy. Plus, several years ago, she had a multi-drug-resistant bacterium that changed her life forever. The statistics were grim; medical reviews said 67 to 83% of people didn't survive it. But I'm a woman of faith. I cried, I fell to my knees and prayed for God to take me instead. He showed up, and she was healed, though it took a long time to recover, and she still deals with some residuals. I don't use that word lightly. She is a living, breathing, walking miracle, and I thank God for her every single day.

So yes, we've always had a strong bond. But nothing prepares you for when your child grows up and moves out. I had helped so many clients through empty-nest grief, but when it happened to me, it rocked me. The silence. The space. The ache. I would go into the room she once inhabited and just remember beautiful moments.

She left for college, and even though I encouraged her to stay in the dorms—because she deserved the full college experience after all the health challenges she'd faced—it was hard. I would smile and cheer her on during the day, then deal with the sadness behind closed doors. If you're a parent, you know.

And now here we were. Both of us are a bit stuck. A bit drained. Both have to adjust to new norms. A bit too comfortable with our routines, but also feeling the weight of isolation.

So that day, we said yes to something small. One outing. One step. A new adventure.

Our first adventure was a charming little coffee shop called Selah, right after one of her baby checkups. It was peaceful and gorgeous with chandeliers adorning the place, and they had menu options that catered to her dietary needs. We took lots of pictures, laughed, and had fun as if we were on vacation. We spoke to the person about how that began, and something shifted inside. It felt light. Free. Joyful.

We put together a video reel and called our Socials *Oklahoma HotSpots* and committed to exploring one to two new places each week to post about. No big expectations—just the joy of doing something different, together, and getting out of the four walls.

What began as healing for our hearts turned into something even bigger.

We posted a few photos and videos. Nothing fancy. Just us being ourselves—real, raw, curious, and joyful. And to our surprise, people started responding. Messages like "Where is this place?" and "Thanks for sharing—this inspired me to get out of the house" started flooding in. Before we knew it, business owners were reaching out asking how much we charged to promote.

Wait. What?

We hadn't thought about charging. We were just sharing from our hearts. But God had a plan, bigger than ours.

My daughter, who was finishing her marketing degree and already doing brand collaborations, was ecstatic. She was really good at it, too. Now, together, we were building a marketing media company. We worked together to create packages that help businesses grow their social media marketing. We started landing clients and building momentum. She even had to hire a small team. And yes, I became one of her team members, too; my daughter is now my boss in that space. It is such an honor to get to watch her shine, stepping more into her calling, and getting to walk beside her.

We were creating something out of nothing—beauty from burnout, connection from isolation, business from brokenness.

Let me be clear, this wasn't just about the fun, cute coffee shop pictures. As a counselor and brain health coach, I know what it looks like when people feel stuck, when depression sets in, when PTSD symptoms increase, and when the anxiety becomes paralyzing. I've worked with military families, trauma survivors, high-level professionals, single moms—you name it. And so many of them describe the same cycle: wake up, do the same thing, feel overwhelmed, so stay inside, go to bed exhausted, repeat.

That's not living. That's surviving, and surviving isn't thriving.

When you isolate, your brain starts to associate safety with solitude, and anything outside of that feels threatening, even new things. Even being around people may feel difficult for some. That's how people get stuck in the cycle of reclusion because the symptoms exacerbate when we don't participate socially. They believe they're protecting themselves, but in reality, they're losing their ability to feel safe in the community.

There's a reason Jesus sent His disciples out in pairs. There's power in partnership. There's safety in connection.

Our weekly outings became beautiful moments and memories. They became our healing space, our therapy, our joy. It felt amazing as it empowered others to get out, and it also helped business owners.

I remember one message that really hit me. A woman wrote, "Since the COVID epidemic, I really don't get out of my house other than work. But after watching your video, I decided to get out and try something new. Thank you." We also had a business employee who said he loved the idea of mother-daughter dates. He said, "Mom is always saying things like 'I miss you,'" and I didn't really know what to do about it, but now I think we could do something like this, and that would be fun. What joy to see how our lives are impacting others, to get out and create a joyful life. That was when we knew this wasn't just a hobby.

And the most beautiful part? My daughter and I were doing this healing, fun journey together.

She's an introvert by nature, highly empathic, sensitive to people's emotions, and with the pregnancy and everything else going on, she needed the joy and fun as much as I did. These outings gave us both something to look forward to. We dreamed again. Laughed again. Played again.

We started discovering new places, meeting incredible business owners, and hearing amazing stories. Stories of resilience, faith, and creativity born out of crisis. We were surrounded by inspiration.

The business is thriving. She's using her gifts to help others grow. We get invited to events, launches, and special community gatherings we would've never known about. Today, we are still having our mother-daughter dates every single week, growing her business, but sometimes with a little one by our side, too.

God took a phone call and turned it into a company. He took our mini vacations and created a major miracle.

And it didn't stop there.

I also began writing a book that God had laid on my heart a long time ago. My book *Breath of Heaven: Manifesting God's Way* began forming out of this season, combining Biblical truth and brain science to help people shift from mess to Masterpiece. In it, I share how I moved from fear and fatigue to peace and purpose and how others can, too.

I even share how my husband and I ended up living on a yacht for a year, building our dream home, becoming debt-free, bringing in wealth, and creating a life we love, all by following the steps God taught me.

Now, my daughter and I are writing a book together with the lessons we've learned. Because this isn't just about us. It's about creating a ripple effect.

So, here's what I want to leave you with: You are not stuck. You are not too far gone. You are not too old, too tired, too sick, or too late. All it takes is one brave step. One phone call. One outing. One yes. You never know what God might do with your willingness.

Your miracle might just be waiting outside your front door. Go create your own amazing life. You never know how amazing it can become.

Sometimes, I reflect back and realize how close I came to staying stuck. How easy it would've been to let fear, fatigue, pain, and comfort win. And honestly, no one would've blamed me. Life after COVID, especially with lingering symptoms, was no joke. Every day felt like pushing a huge wheelbarrow of rocks up a hill. I've learned over the years, and more through this season, that one small action, done in faith, can open a floodgate of blessings.

That's how healing begins. Not with giant leaps, but micro steps. Not with perfect plans, but imperfect yeses. God doesn't ask us to have it all together. He asks us to trust Him with what we have.

And that's what we did. We said yes. We stepped out.

You see, healing is holistic. It's not just the body or mind, it's the spirit, too. We are whole beings, created to thrive in connection, in purpose, and in joy. As a military veteran and someone who grew up with a "suck it up and drive on" mindset, I used to think self-care was a luxury. Something optional. But after what I went through post-COVID, I realized...it's not a luxury. It's a lifeline necessity.

Self-care isn't spa days and bubble baths (though those are lovely). It's asking for help. It's saying no when you're depleted. It's calling your daughter and saying, "Let's do something joyful together." It's choosing life again at whatever level you can. It's creating a joyful life with a new normal.

And that's what I want to encourage in you.

Whether you're in a season of loss, burnout, physical challenges, or transition...whether you feel forgotten, fatigued, or fearful... I want you to know this: There is still beauty ahead. There is still joy waiting to be rediscovered. God is not finished with you.

Maybe your outing won't be to a coffee shop. Maybe it'll be a walk in the park, a drive through the countryside, or an art class you've always wanted to try. The location doesn't matter. The movement does. Healing often comes through motion—physical, emotional, and relational.

The Bible says in Isaiah 43:19 (NIV), "See, I am doing a new thing! Now it springs up; do you not perceive it?" That's the nature of God— He makes rivers in the desert. He brings life out of what looked dead. He turns breakdowns into breakthroughs.

So, here are some gentle action steps you can take today:

1. **Ask yourself:** "What would joy look like right now in my life?" Write it down, even if it feels impossible.
2. **Reach out to someone:** A family member, a friend, a mentor. Don't wait for them to call you; be the one who initiates. Healing starts in connection.
3. **Plan a mini outing:** Just one. It doesn't have to be far or fancy. It just needs to be something that lights your heart up. Something gets you out of your usual space.
4. **Capture the moment:** Take photos, write about it, or even record a short video. You might be surprised how healing it is just to document and reflect on the emotions.

5. **Invite God into it:** Whether it's through prayer, journaling, or quiet gratitude reflection, ask Him to show you how to create a joyful life. He's not only in churches—He's in coffee shops, front porches, and quiet car rides, too.

Looking back now, I realize this wasn't just a mother-daughter journey. It was God answering our prayers. God used our weakness and turned it into a witness. He took our limitations and created something beautiful. He can do it for you, too.

If you're a parent dealing with empty-nest emotions, don't wait for a perfect moment. Create one. If you're someone battling anxiety or post-COVID challenges, give yourself grace and give yourself permission to live again. The road back to joy might not be straight, but it starts with one step.

I often say, "You are a Masterpiece already, just under the mess." That's been true in my life over and over again. And I believe it can be true in yours, too.

Today, I get to share my story, not just through books and business, but through my life as well. I get to have weekly dates with my daughter and now, sweet moments with my grandchildren, too. I get to work in a business born out of love, healing, and creativity. I get to help others manifest God's promises for their lives; nothing brings me more joy.

If you feel inspired by this story and want to take your healing or purpose to the next level, my book *Breath of Heaven: Manifesting God's Way* is filled with the tools, scriptures, brain health insights, and reflection prompts that helped me, and thousands of others transform their lives...from pain into purpose, and fear into faith. You're not alone. And you don't have to figure it all out in one day. Just start. Imagine how beautiful your life can be. You may also be interested in one of my coaching programs. You can find more free resources on the link below.

Your miracle may not come as wrapped presents or grand gestures. It might come in a quiet coffee shop with someone you love. It might come through a photo you take or a story you share that touches someone else's heart.

It might just come the moment you say yes.

So wherever you are today, take a breath. Know that God is not done with your story. Say yes to healing. Yes to joy. Yes to life again.

Because your miracle might be waiting right outside your door.

Be Blessed and Be a Blessing.

Lori Ellen Miller

Soul Journey Secrets LLC
Spiritual Empowerment Pathfinder & Soul Cartographer

https://AllMeByDesign.com
https://www.youtube.com/@SoulJourneySecrets

Lori Ellen Miller is a Spiritual Empowerment Pathfinder, author, and creator of the transformational system, Soul Cartography™. Known for her depth, clarity, and unshakeable belief in the greatness she sees in every woman, Lori guides them to honor their journey and embody who they were born to be. Holding sacred space, she is devoted to helping women align with their higher calling and bring it to life. Her work weaves together Human Design, intuitive guidance, and soul-led strategy to turn struggles into strengths and wounds into wisdom. Whether through her Path of Awakening Retreats that reconnect women with their sacred service, deep 1:1 mentorship, or her Soul-Sync membership, Lori's mission is to liberate women to remember: they are not broken — they are powerful by design. She is the founder of Soul Journey Secrets LLC, and her signature phrase captures her message best: No Pity. No Shame. Just Divine Purpose.

Answering Yes to the Call Within

By Lori Ellen Miller

There's a moment when a whisper becomes a calling.

When an inner nudge feels like a sacred assignment. Something within you begins to stir with excitement and alignment. When you quietly hear, *This is your next step*, even though your mind can't make sense of it yet. You feel this connection to a soul mission that is greater than yourself.

That voice is never loud. It's not forceful. It doesn't always come with a roadmap full of clarity or confidence. Sometimes, it shows up as a flicker in the dark—a quiet sense that you feel within. Something patiently waiting for us to step toward it. And once you've heard it, you can't unhear it.

For me, hearing that voice came many times before I truly listened. For years, I didn't know how to. Before I learned how to connect with spirit and my soul's guidance, I lived mostly from logic—or from reactive emotion. I would make decisions based on what made sense in the moment, or what I thought I was "*supposed*" to do. This mental reasoning sometimes worked out okay, but more often, it didn't. I'd find myself in situations—commitments, relationships, or paths— that were frustrating, complicated, or misaligned. In hindsight, my inner voice had been guiding me all along—I just hadn't learned to trust it yet.

Back then, I didn't yet understand that my soul was always trying to guide me. I saw those experiences as mistakes. Now, I see them as opportunities. Every detour was part of learning to trust. I was just training my "humanness" to surrender to something greater—the nudges of spirit, the quiet knowing of my soul.

Growing up, I wasn't encouraged to take risks or speak my truth. One of my mother's favorite sayings was, "*Don't make waves.*" That message sank in deep. Be quiet. Stay small. Don't stir things up. Maybe then, you'll stay safe. Maybe then, you'll be invisible enough to avoid harm.

Waves or not, harm still found its way in. And for a long time, that fear of being too much—or not enough—kept me trapped in patterns of silence and survival.

But something shifted after my second divorce. I was finally ready to go inward and face myself. The pain I had carried for so long cracked me open. I began to hear the still, quiet voice within—not just hear it, but slowly trust it.

At first, it was a trial-and-error process. Sometimes, I followed it. Sometimes, I didn't. But over time, I realized: Every time I listened, life felt more aligned. Even when it was hard. Especially when it was hard.

Over time, I developed a new relationship with the word "hard." I understand that flow does not mean easy. When I feel myself slipping into a space where it feels hard, I come back to something I wrote once about that word.

When Something Feels Hard

We can tune into the frequency of "hard" in two ways.

- In its low frequency, hard feels like:
  - Having
  - Avoidance
  - Resistance
  - Denial

We avoid, resist, and deny ourselves the potential and possibilities of who we are here to be. We stay in mediocrity, afraid to become more than our current beliefs about who we are and what we're capable of—because the unknown feels harder.

- In its higher frequency, hard becomes:
  - Having
  - Awareness
  - Resilience
  - Dedication

Are we willing to have awareness of the old patterns we're being asked to release to evolve through it?

Are we willing to be resilient, knowing we have what it takes, believing in ourselves, remembering that we've been through hard things before, and trusting that we are not alone?

Are we willing to be dedicated to our evolutionary process and to ourselves, knowing we are worth the effort to take the steps forward?

So, when labeling something as hard, are you asking the powerful question of why it feels that way?

When it comes down to it, it is simply an illusion our mind creates to keep us safe from moving forward because of past patterns. Anytime we feel something is hard, we're being invited into the deeper layers of our soul's calling. We are learning and growing closer to our personal truth. We are presented with an opportunity to release a long-held limitation that we placed upon ourselves.

The mind is not the source of our guidance. It's a tool—a processor—designed to follow the direction of the soul, not dictate it. When the mind takes the lead, it's like letting the computer decide what program to run. When we freeze in indecision or wait for certainty, time keeps moving while we stay stuck. But when we take a step—even a small one, even when it's hard—we're signaling to Spirit that we're not just willing, we're moving forward in radical faith. That's when synchronicities begin to unfold. When we let the soul lead and allow the mind to support that vision, we become unstoppable.

Flow is not about pretending things are easy. It's about alignment. It's about choosing how we engage. It's about saying yes when you don't yet see the path—but you feel the truth of it and trust the process. Trust is knowing that even when the road is unclear, you are not walking it alone. That every step you take in faith activates unseen support.

The more I said yes to those inner nudges, the more I could feel joy returning—joy that wasn't based on external conditions, but one that rose up from the inside out. Each step required courage. Not perfection. Not having it all figured out. Through willingness and an action step, I became more myself.

When I was building a business based on deep spiritual work, I found myself once again standing on the edge of something I couldn't quite explain. I had taken all the business-building courses. I had followed the advice of the "gurus." And yet, something inside me said... *this isn't your way.*

I had spent years healing from trauma, reclaiming my voice, and empowering other women to remember who they truly are. I had found purpose in that path. But even with all I had overcome and created, there was still something stirring deep within me—an invitation to rise into something even bigger.

That invitation didn't come with instructions. It came with questions.

What if I'm not ready?
What if I don't know how?
What if this is too big for me?

But none of it unfolds if we stay in our heads. When we're caught in the cycle of "how," "should," "need," or "when," we are swimming against the flow. These words may sound responsible, but they are based upon fear. They come from the belief that we must control or earn what's already meant for us. When we drop those words from our vocabulary, we open ourselves to the energy of infinite possibilities.

The challenge is that our mind will almost always try to stop us. It will say:

But how will you make it happen?
What if it doesn't work?
Shouldn't you wait until you're more prepared?
You need more information first.
When the timing is right, then you can begin.

But those words—how, what, should, need, when—are not guidance.

They're delay tactics disguised as logic.

They're the voice of fear wearing the mask of reason.

Doubts may creep in from time to time, derived from old habits. The mind has its ways to avoid the unknown, encouraged by former limiting beliefs.

Oh no, can I really do this?
What if I don't know enough?
How will I pull it all together?

I didn't have the answers. But I had a choice. I chose to trust that when the soul speaks, it whispers. It speaks in nudges, with curiosity, and in truth, wrapped in the kind of discomfort that invites growth.

When I veered back into my head, trying to figure it all out and trying to make it work, it started to feel heavy. Then I remembered to be still, listen to the whisper within, and surrender once again. I let go of how it "should" look. I stopped chasing answers. And I leaned back into the flow of spirit.

At first, it looked like nothing was happening. But one thing led to another—often in ways that didn't seem connected. Still, I followed the breadcrumbs. Eventually, the pieces started clicking into place.

This calling was to lead retreats in Thailand. It felt like a thread woven into my soul's mission—an expansive vision that both lit me up and scared me at the same time. It required me to stretch beyond what I had done before. It asked me to release the idea that I needed to know all the steps before I began. And it invited me to trust that the unknown wasn't something to fear—but something to befriend. This was bigger than anything I'd done before. But it felt right. In my gut, there was this buzzing joy—like my soul was doing a happy dance.

So, I took a soul-led step—rooted in trust and guided by what lit me up. I let the Universe know I was serious—not with words, but with action. I committed to Thai language lessons—even without retreat dates, a venue, or a mapped-out plan.

It was a simple step, but it shifted the energy instantly and opened a flow I could never have predicted. I followed the nudge to find a tutor, and after a few misaligned attempts, I found her. The moment we met, I felt an immediate yes—and so did she. A few weeks later, she mentioned another student who runs retreats in Thailand and offered to connect us. Then, as if the Universe was winking, she shared that her brother is a guide in Northern Thailand—in one of the provinces I had already dreamed of visiting.

Then, doors that once seemed invisible began to open—not because I forced them, but because I aligned with them through action. That's the part no one talks about. Being aligned is one thing... Taking action is the key. It's like stepping into the current of your soul's flow toward your destination. Flow is not passive. It's an active partnership with the Universe. It asks us to move—not because we know the outcome, but because we trust the process. Every time I've stepped into the unknown with aligned action, the Universe has responded.

Be gentle with yourself. Something I often say to my clients: *If you already know how to do it, it's probably not big enough. The soul rarely calls you to what you've already mastered.*

It calls you to be who you truly are, not who you've been conditioned to be or who you've told yourself you need to be. And this is unfamiliar terrain.

When fear shows up now, remember: there was a time you didn't know how to walk. You didn't know what would happen when you stood. You would fall, get back up, and do it all over again. But you kept going. And now, walking is second nature. You don't even have to think about it. You may not remember those days of learning to walk, but you know you did it. That same resilience exists in you now, for anything that you choose to take on.

I've come to believe that we each have soul agreements—assignments we chose before we arrived. The callings we feel are echoes of those agreements, pulling us toward our highest expression. And when we say yes to them, we begin to remember who we are. We begin to lead, serve, and create from our Truest Self.

By saying yes to my own soul's call, I've witnessed the ripple effect. The women I've served didn't just receive tools or guidance; They felt seen, liberated, and reconnected to their own power. They embraced all parts of themselves—their past, their pain, their truth—and turned them into fuel for their authentic expression. They no longer question if their voice matters. They know it does. They're no longer afraid of their story. It's become a foundation for them to stand on and own who they are.

If I had stayed in my comfort zone, I would've stayed small. And the women I now walk beside—women awakening to their own truth— may never have found their way to me.

So let me ask you something:

What is your yes calling you toward?

What's been tugging at your soul, waiting for you to stop asking "how" and start trusting what's already yours?

You don't have to know every step. You don't have to feel ready. You just have to say yes. From your heart. And then move.

Because your next chapter isn't waiting to be discovered—it's waiting to be written. And it will be written by the version of you who's bold enough to say yes to what scares you—because it's also what lights you up.

When you feel that nudge—that pull toward something bigger—It's your soul saying: *This is who you came here to be.*

So yes, it may feel scary.

Yes, you may have doubts.

But remember: It wouldn't have come to you if it wasn't meant for you.

Step outside the comfort zone. Or even the "uncomfort zone" that feels familiar but no longer serves you. Say yes to the vision that makes your gut dance and your spirit come alive. Trust that the support, the people, and the path will unfold as you walk it.

The bigger the calling, the more it requires surrender. It asks us to trust what we cannot yet see, to follow with faith, and to remember that expansion lives through it.

Sometimes, people ask me how I learned to live this way—to trust without knowing, to say yes before I felt ready. The honest answer? I started paying attention to the nudges.

I stopped waiting for perfect conditions because the moment we take one aligned step, life meets us there. But none of that can happen if we're still waiting to feel ready. There's a rhythm to the Universe that responds to courage. And that rhythm requires movement.

When we say yes to a calling that stretches us, we aren't just stepping into something new—we are evolving into someone new. Or...

maybe not new at all—maybe we're just remembering who we've always been, before the world told us to play small.

And that journey takes dedication.

It takes resilience.

It takes awareness of the stories we've outgrown and the truth trying to rise within us.

The truth is, the next chapter of our lives isn't waiting to be discovered.

It's waiting to be written—by us.

We write it by choosing.

By answering the call within.

By taking one sacred step at a time, even when we don't know the entire path.

That's what unleashing her means.

Not becoming someone else. But finally allowing who you've always been to lead.

She's not waiting for permission... The only thing she's waiting for... is your yes.

You have everything you need to begin.

You are not here to play small.

You are here to unleash her.

And the moment you say yes—not just with your words, but with action—the Universe will rise to meet you.

Stacey Dori Garel

CEO of Gifted Administrative Services

www.linkedin.com/in/staceygarel
https://www.facebook.com/stacey2qute
https://www.instagram.com/iamstaceydori/
https://www.giftedadministrativeservices.com
https://www.yourspiritualgoddess.com

Stacey is also a certified Event Manager with an extensive background in managing large events. With over 15 years of Corporate Event Management & Tradeshow experience. Stacey has worked for Fortune 500 companies providing focus of executing superior brand experience. Stacey has managed over 1,000's of National Tradeshows, Events, and conferences. Stacey's excellent customer service and event experience lead her to serve as an Event planner for the 2012 Democratic National Convention, and 2013 Super Bowl. Stacey focuses on marketing, technology, and branding. Bringing creativity, and excellent leadership skills to all Events and Tradeshows. Stacey Garel is an Bestselling published author with the 9 times best selling book Peeling Off The Layers To Unmask New Beginnings. In 2023 Stacey was nominated for a RICE Award as Founder's Rising Star. In 2023 she received and Outstanding Citizen Award from her home state of Georgia. In 2025 she received a resolution from the State of GA for her outstanding accomplishments & community service. Stacey is an active motional speaker & leader in her community

Reclaiming Our Power in Faith: The Journey to Self-Love

By Stacey Dori Garel

As women, we often find ourselves navigating through a world filled with expectations, judgments, and comparisons. The struggle to love ourselves can feel like an uphill battle, especially when external voices drown out the inner whispers of our worth. In this chapter, I want to share my journey of reclaiming my power in faith and how it has helped me overcome the challenges of self-love.

Growing up, I believed that my values were tied to my achievements and my ability to please others. I remember being praised for my grades, my spiritual abilities, and my willingness to put others first. While these accolades felt good in that moment, they also created a silent pressure to maintain a certain image—a façade that I thought defined my worth.

I faced many challenges on my path to self-love. There were moments of self-doubt that crept in like shadows, whispering lies that I wasn't good enough. In my personal life, the struggle for self-love took on a different form. Relationships, whether romantic or platonic, became arenas where my worth was tested. I found myself seeking validation from others, hoping that their acceptance would fill the void I felt within. I remember dating someone who didn't fully appreciate who I was, often making comments that left me questioning my beauty and my worth. It was a painful lesson, but it was also a turning point. I realized that I had been giving away my power to others instead of standing firm in my identity.

Faith became my anchor during these tumultuous times. I sought solace in Scripture, finding verses that reminded me of my inherent worth. One of my favorites became Psalm 139:14: "I praise you because I am fearfully and wonderfully made; your works are wonderful, I know that full well." This verse resonated deeply with me, reinforcing the idea that my value is not determined by others but by the Creator who made me. It was in these moments of reflection and prayer that I began to reclaim my power.

As I leaned into my faith, I discovered the importance of self-acceptance. I learned that loving myself was not selfish; rather, it was an essential part of my journey. I began to affirm my worth daily, speaking life into my dreams and aspirations. I remember standing in front of the mirror, looking into my own eyes, and declaring, "I am enough. I am worthy of love and success." At first, it felt foreign, but over time, those affirmations became a powerful tool in reshaping my mindset.

One of the most significant challenges I faced was in the corporate world, the need to prove myself constantly. I often felt the pressure to excel beyond my peers to gain respect and recognition. This led to a relentless pursuit of perfection, which took a toll on my mental and emotional well-being. I remember spending late nights at the office, sacrificing my personal time in pursuit of validation. I was caught in a cycle of overwork, convinced that my worth was tied to my achievements.

In moments of exhaustion, I turned to my faith for guidance. I sought wisdom in prayer and reflection, asking God to help me find balance. I realized that success does not solely define me; rather, it is a part of my journey. I began to understand that my worth is inherent, not contingent on accolades or titles. This shift in perspective was liberating. I learned to celebrate my achievements without losing sight of my identity.

It was a pivotal moment in my faith journey that led me to understand the importance of reclaiming my power. I began to explore the Scriptures, seeking comfort and guidance from the Word of God. I discovered verses that spoke directly to my heart, reminding me that I am fearfully and wonderfully made (Psalm 139:14) and that my worth is not determined by the world's standards but by God.

As I immersed myself in faith, I discovered a growing sense of empowerment. I learned that self-love is not a destination but a journey—one that requires patience, grace, and a willingness to confront the lies that had held me captive for so long. I started to see my flaws not as failures but as opportunities for growth. I began to embrace the parts of myself that I had previously deemed unworthy, recognizing that they were integral to my unique story.

The process of reclaiming my power in faith involved a lot of soul-searching. I had to confront the negative self-talk that had become so ingrained in my mind. I began practicing affirmations, speaking truths over myself that aligned with what God says about me. I would look in the mirror and declare with conviction, "I am enough. I am loved. I am worthy of all the good things life has to offer." At first, it felt strange, almost like I was trying on a new outfit that didn't quite fit. But with time, those affirmations became a part of my daily routine, reshaping my thoughts and beliefs.

Another challenge I faced was the need for community. I realized that I couldn't do this alone. I needed the support and encouragement of other women who were on similar journeys. I began to seek out friendships with those who uplifted me, who spoke life into my dreams, and who held me accountable in my pursuit of self-love. Together, we shared our struggles, our victories, and our prayers, creating a safe space where we could be vulnerable and honest. I also created a livestream show on Facebook called Goddess Talk with Stacey Dori to help encourage women and give spiritual insight.

In this community and my livestream show, I found solace in the fact that I was not alone in my struggles. Many women shared their own stories of insecurity and self-doubt. It was liberating to hear that we all faced challenges in loving ourselves, and it reinforced the idea that self-love is a collective journey. We began to celebrate each other's victories, no matter how small, and that sense of camaraderie fueled our individual pursuits of self-acceptance.

One of the most transformative aspects of reclaiming my power was learning to let go of perfectionism. I had to remind myself that I am a work in progress, and that's perfectly okay. I began to approach life with a sense of curiosity rather than judgment. I allowed myself to make mistakes, to stumble and fall, and to rise again with renewed determination. Through this process, I discovered that my imperfections were not something to be ashamed of but rather a testament to my resilience and growth.

As I deepened my relationship with God, I found that the more I leaned into my faith, the more I was able to silence the negative voices in my head. I learned to pray fervently, asking for strength and guidance as I navigated the complexities of self-love. I found peace in the understanding that I am not defined by my past mistakes or by the opinions of others. My worth is rooted in my identity as a child of God.

In this journey, I also learned the importance of self-care. I realized that taking time for myself was not selfish but necessary. I began to prioritize activities that nourished my body, mind, and spirit. Whether it was through journaling, exercising, or simply taking a moment to breathe deeply, I found that these practices helped me reconnect with myself. I learned to listen to my needs and honor them, recognizing that self-love is an intentional act of self-respect.

As I continued to grow in my faith, I began to see self-love as an act of worship. By choosing to love myself, I was honoring God, who created me in His image. I learned that it is not only okay to love myself but that it is essential for living a fulfilled and purpose-driven life. I began to understand that when I embrace my worth, I am better equipped to serve and love others.

Now, when challenges arise, I remind myself of the power of faith. I hold onto the promises that God has for me, knowing that I am never alone in my struggles. I lean into prayer and seek guidance, trusting that each step I take is part of a greater plan. I celebrate my progress, acknowledging that the journey of self-love is ongoing and that it is okay to have ups and downs.

As I conclude this chapter, I want to encourage all readers to embark on their own journey of reclaiming their power in faith. Embrace the beautiful, unique person that you are. Recognize the challenges you face as opportunities for growth. Surround yourself with a supportive community that uplifts you, and do not shy away from self-care. Remember that self-love is not a destination but a journey—one that is filled with grace, patience, and unwavering faith.

Together, let us reclaim our power, rise above self-doubt, and embrace the incredible women we are meant to be. Let us walk in faith, knowing that we are worthy of love and that self-love is an essential part of our beautiful journey.

This chapter is a call to action for every woman to embrace her worth and reclaim her power through faith. It's an invitation to start a transformative journey towards self-love, guided by the understanding that we are all beautifully made and deserving of love—both from ourselves and from others. I want everyone to know that everything you want in life belongs to you! Say this daily, as God has already provided a table for you. Remember to keep the faith, but most importantly, embrace your power. Keep your light shining, never let anyone dim what God so proudly gave to you. Let us walk in faith, knowing that we are deserving of love and acceptance, both from ourselves and from the world around us.

As we navigate the complexities of life, may we always remember that we are fearfully and wonderfully made, and that our stories are worthy of being told. Let's speak of the power of our lives, lifting each other up as we journey together toward self-love and acceptance.

Shraddha Chandwadkar

Certified Self Esteem and Brain Health Coach

www.linkedin.com/in/shraddhachandwadkar
https://www.facebook.com/shraddha.chandwadkar
www.instagram.com/luminouslifelabs
www.shraddhachandwadkar.com

Shraddha Chandwadkar is a certified Self-esteem coach and Dr. Amen certified Brain Health Professional. Her workshops, coaching sessions, focus on practical strategies to improve brain health, boost confidence, overcome self-doubt, increase self- awareness and develop a positive mindset for women and children. Shraddha has coauthored four bestselling anthologies "Becoming an Unstoppable Woman in Health and Wellness Part 2," "Pray Don't Panic," "She Wins Nice Girls Finish First," and "Letters to Him." She is a Reiki Master and a volunteer executive program director at a yoga and wellness non-profit. She received the 'President Volunteer Service Award' in 2024 acknowledging her service. Shraddha is a mother and a spiritual seeker who loves to spend quality time in meditative & contemplative practices. An Engineer by education, Shraddha has an MS, in Computer Engineering, from NC State University USA, and Bachelor in Electronics Engineering from Pune, India.

Unleash The "Real" You

By Shraddha Chandwadkar

When you stand before the looking glass, whose presence truly manifests? Is your gaze drawn to the physical tapestry – the delicate threads of fine lines, the wisdom etched in wrinkles, the sun's kisses in freckles, the spectrum of your skin, and the crafted illusion of makeup? Or do you feel the nascent stirrings of a soul, patiently awaiting release, or perhaps already soaring unburdened? Do you truly listen to the quiet counsel of your inner voice? Does it playfully echo, "Knock, knock, who are you?" When we confine our self-perception to the mere labels of "girl" or "woman," our focus often narrows to superficialities: our gender and physical form. This limited perspective can foster self-doubt, fear of failure, a perpetual need for external validation, and diminished self-esteem, ultimately leaving us feeling trapped. To genuinely flourish, we must transcend these restrictive identities by shedding the beliefs, patterns, and tendencies that construct our self-imposed prisons. Though initially daunting, this deeper introspection allows our true inner selves to radiate.

The journey of life is a powerful teacher, and every person we meet holds a lesson for us. But are we truly learning? Are we doing the necessary inner work? To unleash our authentic inner Self, we must actively pursue our freedom. So, what exactly is this freedom? It is not about staying out late partying or constantly buying new things. Instead, it is about connecting with our true selves and gradually shedding the negative patterns, beliefs, and habits that hold us back. It means rising above the clouded thoughts of the mind and blossoming from within, just like beautiful lotuses emerge from murky water.

This leads us to ask: How do we bloom when life feels difficult? How do we face our ingrained patterns? And how do we change the stories we tell ourselves?

Here are several strategies to help unleash your inner beauty.

Discovering Your Core Purpose

As a student, my primary "why?" revolved around academic excellence to secure a fulfilling career and stable livelihood. Upon marriage, my focus naturally transitioned to cultivating a blissful family life and raising healthy, joyful children. However, through deeper introspection and guidance from numerous spiritual masters, I came to understand a more profound purpose underpinning these objectives. This true purpose involves directly confronting and challenging the false identity, along with the negative thought patterns, tendencies, and vices that originate from it. It is about grasping our authentic selves, comprehending the essence of self-love, and recognizing the nature of self-doubt. Only by understanding both facets of this coin can we truly transcend our limitations. This means perceiving ourselves beyond the confines of body and mind, and experiencing our true state of being. This renewed, higher purpose now empowers me to navigate life's challenges with unwavering clarity.

Self-Awareness

Once you have identified your purpose, the next crucial step is to cultivate self-awareness. It is estimated that a staggering 50,000 to 70,000 thoughts stream through our minds daily, with 90% of them being repetitive. This begs the question: Are these thoughts serving your purpose, or are they pulling you into self-pity and victimhood?

It is vital to remember that not every thought deserves your belief. Practices like mindfulness, meditation, and self-inquiry offer powerful pathways to deepen self-awareness. As you become self-aware, you will be better equipped to identify the thoughts, feelings, patterns, speech, and actions that hinder your growth. This heightened awareness also allows you to recognize your strengths and weaknesses, a process greatly aided by daily reflective journaling.

I leverage daily contemplation, mindfulness, meditation, and Kriya yoga techniques to enhance my self-awareness. These spiritual practices, known as sadhana, have been learned from various spiritual masters, including Tejguru Sirshree, founder of Tejgyan Foundation in Pune, India, and Paramahamsa Prajnanananda, spiritual head of Kriya Yoga Institute.

Growth Mindset

Every challenge I have encountered in life has been a profound learning experience, solidifying my boundaries and unleashing my boundless potential. Embracing the understanding that failures pave the way to success is fundamental to cultivating a growth mindset. Though I have faced setbacks as a student and an entrepreneur, I have come to realize that I haven't truly failed. Each perceived failure has simply opened a new door, presenting a fresh challenge that I have eagerly embraced.

Failure, I have learned, is always pregnant with solutions; we just need to develop the vision to see them. This clarity comes only through confronting challenges with honesty and courage, recognizing that future setbacks are always a possibility.

I have been fortunate to witness my parents navigate their own obstacles head-on. My father, for instance, bravely overcame alcoholism by embracing vulnerability and seeking help, a journey my mother steadfastly supported during his darkest hours. They modeled how to face adversity rather than succumbing to escape or the "why me?" trap. These formative experiences profoundly shape my own development of a growth mindset.

Identifying Negative Self-Talk

Do you ever hear your inner critic? What does it say to you? Does it whisper, "I am not worthy," "I am not brave," "I am not loved," "I am not enough," "I am poor," "I am always sick," "Nobody loves me," or "Why do I have to face this"? Negative self-talk perpetuates a self-sabotaging cycle. Daily affirmations and shifting your internal narrative can transform this negative self-talk into positive one.

Changing Your Narrative

Changing your narrative is like rewriting the script of your inner critic. Instead of repeating old, unhelpful stories – "I am not good enough" or "I always mess up" – you consciously choose to replace them with new, empowering ones. This shift is not about ignoring reality, but about focusing on your strengths, progress, and potential. It is actively choosing to tell yourself a story of growth and capability, which then shapes your feelings and actions.

Write down these affirmations in a journal as a daily ritual to change your narrative.

I am worthy

I am loved

I am brave

I am enough

I complete all my tasks on time.

I am wealthy

I am healthy

Believing in Yourself

Have Faith in yourself. This isn't just a feel-good platitude; it is a fundamental belief in your own capabilities and resilience. Life will inevitably throw obstacles your way, but instead of viewing them as insurmountable barriers, see them as opportunities for growth.

Every roadblock you encounter isn't there to stop you; it is there to strengthen you, forcing you to find new paths, develop new skills, and discover inner reserves you didn't know you had.

Similarly, every challenge you face isn't meant to defeat you; it is designed to uplift you. When weight lifters work out in a gym, they lift heavy weights not to be crushed, but to build muscle and become stronger. Challenges work in the same way, pushing you beyond your comfort zone and helping you realize your true potential.

And those moments where you feel constrained or held back, those shackles? They are not meant to keep you bound. Instead, they are there to help you identify what is holding you back, giving you the impetus to unleash your true self and break free from limitations, whether they are external circumstances or self-imposed beliefs.

One of the biggest traps people fall into is constantly worrying about external validation. This means letting your actions, choices, and even your self-worth be dictated by "what will people feel or say or think?" This shifts your focus away from your own internal compass. When you seek validation from others, you are constantly chasing approval, which can lead to insecurity, indecision, and a loss of your own identity.

The key is to be true to yourself. This means understanding your values, passions, and convictions and then living in alignment with them, regardless of what others might expect or desire. When you are your authentic self, you build genuine confidence that comes from within. In essence, trusting yourself and your journey is the ultimate act of liberation.

Continuous Learning

Cultivate a love for learning; it is an invaluable asset. Since arriving in the U.S., I have prioritized learning over watching TV or wasting my time unnecessarily. After completing my master's in computer engineering, I couldn't work because I was on an H4 visa, which prohibited me from working. My son was born a couple of weeks after my master's graduation. I spent time with him, grew a vegetable garden, and attended several discourses by a spiritual master of the Ashtavakra Gita. That was the beginning of my spiritual journey. I also learned Reiki and began offering complementary Reiki healing sessions to my friends and family. Additionally, I took cake decorating lessons at Michaels craft store and baked and decorated several cakes for my friends and family. After receiving my green card, I spent some years working as a patent analyst. A move to a different state, coupled with my children being small and my husband's travel, led me to step back from my career. However, I didn't stop exploring. I launched an organic food e-store but quickly realized the significant capital required for marketing and the intense competition. Around the same time, we discovered real estate entrepreneurship, delving into strategies like wholesaling and short sales. We educated ourselves through Rich Dad education and began this as a side business.

I have always had a deep thirst for spiritual and personal development. Since 2009, I have consistently listened to discourses of my spiritual enlightened master, Tejguru Sirshree, every week. In 2019, I further deepened this commitment by adding Kriya Yoga practice from Paramahamsa Prajnanananda. This practice, with its focus on breath, has become especially significant for me; post-COVID, I truly believe everyone should explore Kriya Yoga for its profound health and spiritual benefits in addition to the contemplation and understanding from Tejguru Sirshree's practices. Beyond these, since 2015, I have pursued numerous certifications including Life Coaching, Self-Esteem Coaching, Trauma-Informed Coaching, Relationship Coaching, Emotional Intelligence, Emotional Freedom Technique, and most recently, on my way to complete the Brain Health Coaching. In addition to these endeavors, I have contributed chapters to four anthologies, with this as my fifth. I am also working on my own solo books. My passion for learning is insatiable, and I intend to continue expanding my knowledge.

Service

Prioritizing time for personal development and growth is crucial, but extending that time to others elevates the journey further. While I cherish learning and being present for my family, I also make it a point to give back to the community through various non-profit endeavors. In the past, I have volunteered as a memory and mind science assistant coach for a social enterprise. Now, I serve as an Executive Program Director at a yoga and wellness non-profit, which is dedicated to offering free yoga and wellness workshops to the community. Additionally, I volunteer with spiritual organizations, like contributing to translation or editing books, or hosting and organizing retreats and meditation sessions. This service not only brings me a deep sense of contentment but also nurtures feelings of compassion and devotion.

Resources on the Path

Coaches & Mentors

As we embark on a path of self-enquiry or self-awareness, the guidance of a spiritual mentor, coach, or someone who has already navigated this journey can become invaluable. There is always someone who has walked the path before us. Do not hesitate to seek help from those who can hold your hand, illuminate the way, and assist you in exploring your inner layers. Throughout my own life journey, I have had the privilege of encountering several healing masters, enlightened spiritual masters like Tejguru Sirshree, Paramahamsa Prajnanananda, Sri Sri Ravi Shankar, Guru Karunamaya, to name a few, and self-help coaches whose teachings have been instrumental in helping me unlearn limiting beliefs and unleash my true potential.

Books

Consider self-help, self-development, and leadership books as essential guides in your quest to unleash your true self. Books that have helped me in my self development journey are *The Source, The Unshaken Mind* and *The Warrior's Mirror* by Sirshree, *You Can Heal Your Life* by Louise Hay, *Autobiography of a Yogi* by Paramahansa Yogananda, *Apprenticed to a Himalayan Master* by Sri M, *The Placebo* by Dr. Joe Dispenza, *Dying to Be Me* by Anita Moorjani and many many more.

Courses

The internet has revolutionized learning, offering countless online courses. I have taken full advantage, earning certifications in different self-help areas. Now, I am passionate about sharing what I have learned as a life, self-esteem, and Brain Health Coach for women, teens, and children.

I feel immense gratitude for the chance to pass on the lessons I have learned throughout my journey. My sincere hope is that this resonates with you and empowers you to discover and unleash your true potential. I wish you the best in your journey in unleashing the "real" you.

Gina Marisa

Gina Marisa Wellness
Transplant Wellness Specialist

https://www.linkedin.com/in/gina-marisa-683534ba/
https://www.facebook.com/gina.marisa.581
https://www.ginamarisa.com/

Gina is a Transplant Wellness Specialist who helps organ transplant recipients enhance their post-transplant wellbeing so they can maintain optimal health, minimize side effects, and embrace their second chance at life with confidence. Her journey toward health began when she discovered she was in renal failure, leading to a life-saving kidney transplant over 30 years ago. This experience inspired her to prioritize good health. Gina is a yoga teacher and a Level II Reiki practitioner. She is a self-proclaimed "wellness junkie", a lifelong learner, and enjoys writing, traveling, photography, and hiking.

Midlife Without Crisis: From Comfort to Courage

By Gina Marisa

I didn't know it at the time, but turning 50 was the spark that ignited my metamorphosis. In the past seven years, I have stretched myself like a dormant muscle finally remembered, growing more in this short span than during the half-century that preceded it. Each experience that pushed me beyond my comfort zone has polished away the layers of caution and conformity I'd carefully cultivated. What I have also discovered, to my profound surprise, is that I now hunger for that edge of discomfort.

The Catalyst—Hawaii

Ever since I was a little girl, I have wanted to go to Hawaii. I can't explain why, but I just knew I needed to go. It has been number one on my bucket list since I can remember.

You might be thinking, "How is Hawaii a stretch?" The first challenge was the flight from Florida—my stomach lurching with every air pocket, my body's lifelong betrayal of motion sickness threatening to ruin the journey before it began. The mere thought of boat excursions filled me with dread, memories of past seasickness episodes leaving a bitter taste in my mouth. These physical reactions had imprisoned me geographically for decades. But the islands called to me with a voice louder than my fears, and I was finally willing to endure whatever discomfort was necessary to fulfill this lifelong dream.

One of the first things we did was drive the Road to Hana in Maui. I've never held my breath for such a long time! Why? The Road to Hana is practically one lane with two-way traffic and no shoulder. The views are absolutely stunning, if you dare look. The other scary thing about the drive was the locals. They weave in and out of traffic at an alarming speed without a care in the world. I seriously thought I was going to die on that road!

The other thing we did in Maui was walk through a bamboo forest. The extremely tall bamboo reached to the sky like ancient sentinels, their hollow stalks creaking and whispering in the gentle breeze. At the end of the forest stood a magnificent waterfall, but there was a sign that read Do Not Pass This Point Fatalities Have Occurred— Violating a Closure: $100. I was ready to turn around, my rule-following instincts kicking in, but my boyfriend decided he wanted to go. I contemplated it for a few minutes, my heart pounding in my chest as I weighed decades of cautious decision-making against this potential moment of joy. Finally, with a deep breath that felt like inhaling courage itself, I decided what the heck—I'm in Hawaii. I'm doing this. The pounding in my chest slowly subsided as I stepped beyond the warning sign. I was no longer a "good girl."

Kauai was next, and it was definitely my favorite. Our main excursion on this island was a jaunt on a 24' rigid hull raft along the Na Pali coast to a private village. The speedboat stopped about 20 minutes in so that we could do some snorkeling. Remember how I get seasick? In order to overcome this, I put peppermint essential oil behind my ears and in my water and drank it continuously. I did not do any scuba diving, though. I just sat on the boat staring at the deep blue, clear water. Sitting probably wasn't the best decision, but I had already decided that I wasn't going in. Once snorkeling was over, we took the boat to the private area. I think because the boat was so fast skidding over the waves like an ambitious child doing hopscotch, I hardly felt any motion, so no motion sickness—win!

Overall, the trip was amazing, and I am so glad that I didn't let my motion sickness stop me from creating fond memories.

Finding Alignment

My next crazy move was becoming a yoga teacher. In the 10 years prior to deciding to take this leap, I had been captivated by the transformations I witnessed in others—listening to their animated stories of self-discovery and watching their bodies and spirits change. These yogis described experiences that seemed almost mystical to me, such as finding their purpose, learning to manage stress, and achieving moments of clarity they called enlightenment. I, too, yearned for those same experiences.

My training group was small, only six people, but as I scanned the small room, I became acutely aware that I was the oldest. Not only that, but I could have been a mom to three of them! I began to wonder if I had made a mistake going down this path. Limiting beliefs began to emerge... Was I strong enough? Could I really teach others? Would I have time to do this as a single mom? (Two hundred hours in six months with a job and a child is more than you think!) Did I just waste a bunch of money on something I may not be able to complete? But I was determined to make it work.

What I learned is that I was strong enough. And not just physically, but in all the ways that truly matter. In fact, training made me physically stronger—bonus! It was tough in the beginning because I was sore ALL the time—a deep, persistent ache throughout my entire body that followed me like a shadow. Even simple movements like getting out of bed or reaching for a coffee mug were surprisingly challenging.

Another area that stretched me was teaching. If you've ever been to a yoga class, you know that the teacher is in the front of the room, and the students are spread out in front of her—much like a speaker giving a speech to an audience. I was petrified the first time I had to do a teach-back. Fortunately, I had lots of practice in front of my five peers. Today, I have no problem teaching yoga classes.

Teaching yoga has been one of the best experiences since turning 50. It has given my life so much more depth and appreciation for my body than I could have imagined.

Time for Adventure

If you had told me 20 years ago that I would be driving a 24-foot RV, I would have said, "There's no way in hell I'm driving something that big!" And yet, as I sit here writing about this chapter of my life, I've been doing just that for four years.

I'm not really sure how the idea came to be, but one day in May or June of 2020, I popped my head out of the door of my bedroom and said to my boyfriend, "What do you think about selling everything and moving into an RV full-time?" The weird thing about this statement was that we didn't have cable at the time, so I had no idea the RV lifestyle was a big thing.

By November 2020, I purchased Rio (apparently RVs get names just like boats), and in March 2021, we sold the house and most of our stuff, save for a small amount in a storage unit, and were on the road to our first gig in Tennessee. My friends and family thought I was crazy. I can't really blame them, though. I lived my entire life as that good girl.

During our RV research, we learned that workcamping is one way to live on the road. The premise behind workcamping is that you volunteer your time, usually 20-30 hours a week, in exchange for a free campsite. We decided this would be a great way to travel without going bankrupt paying for campsites.

I had a few goals in mind for this particular lifestyle. First, I wanted to see as much of my beautiful country, the United States, as possible. I would love to visit all 48 contiguous states and discover as much beauty as I can. Second, I wanted to try new things and have the word "adventure" as my middle name. Thus far, I have taken my first hot air balloon ride, participated as an extra on a TV pilot set, stayed overnight on an alpaca farm, sat in the U.S. and Canada at the same time, worked on an herb farm, and many more. Third, since I'm a people person, I wanted to meet new people. We've met many and have remained in contact with a few. Finally, I wanted new and different food experiences. And by new, I mean no chain restaurants. Our favorite places so far have been Raleigh for the restaurant scene (they also have an amazing farmers market!) and Vermont for food (best bacon and asparagus I've ever had, as well as the maple creemee).

While it may seem glamorous, the RV lifestyle is not without its challenges. We've been kicked out of three workcamping gigs, slept in the "dining room" for a night, had the jacks fail (leaving us tilted at a nauseating angle), hit the side of a narrow mountain road, had two recalls that took forever to complete because not all dealers can accommodate RVs, and several more. Through each crisis, we've learned to breathe through the stress, to find humor in the absurd, and to appreciate a spectacular sunset or two that somehow makes it all worthwhile.

Breaking Free

At the end of 2023, I took part in a business challenge. It was eight weeks long and ended January 5, 2024. Each week, we had homework to complete, and every Friday was a live call with the instructor, Dr. Benjamin Hardy, an organizational psychologist, during which he would teach and then open it up to questions and give advice. I paid a lot of money for this challenge, so I was very diligent about completing the homework and attending the calls. On the last Friday of the challenge, there were about 200 people on the call. I had not previously participated in any of the question/advice portion of the calls, but on this day, I had a question and just knew he was going to call on me. So much so that I had my cursor hovering over the unmute button.

After giving advice to three people, he called on me. I mentioned that I knew what my 80% was that was holding me back but wasn't sure how to move forward. When he asked what my 80% was, I said, "My job." He then proceeded to give me some advice for about five minutes, and then he posed a bombshell question—"So why don't you quit your job? Commit here in front of all of these people." When I shockingly agreed, he then said, "Do it today." Tears streamed down my face. I had been wanting to leave my job of 33 years for a good 15 years but felt paralyzed. My job was secure; it provided a decent salary, health and dental insurance, and stability. It also allowed me the freedom to work remotely for 30 hours a week.

But those really weren't good reasons to hold me there. In fact, I felt stifled. What really held me there was fear—fear of the unknown. Over the last 20 years, I've done a lot of inner work, and deep inside, I knew those weren't good reasons to stay at a job that no longer fulfilled me. When challenged by Dr. Hardy to "quit today," everything came rushing in, and I said, "Ok, I will." That was Friday at 1:30 p.m. Since I wasn't in town at the time, I decided to make an appointment with both of my bosses for the following week so that I could tell them in person. When I got there, I had a whole speech planned but didn't get past the first sentence, "I've decided to retire," before my boss said, "Yeah, I had a feeling." From there, it was a very cordial discussion. As I drove out of the parking lot for the final time, I felt a huge relief flood through my entire body in waves of tingling warmth. It was as if someone had removed a giant boulder off the top of my head, and my body was suddenly released from invisible chains.

As I drove toward an unscripted future that was finally, gloriously mine, I realized that retiring from my job was the most difficult thing I've ever done, but also the most freeing.

Building Anew

One big reason I wanted to leave my job was that I really wanted to start my own wellness business. Ever since my kidney transplant over 31 years ago, I have been very passionate about staying healthy. But it's more than that. Each time I learn something new, I want to share it with everyone because "you don't know what you don't know." I've done so much research on how to stay healthy and thriving, and I'm doing a great job at it. Two of my health goals are to live to be a healthy 100-year-old and the longest-lived kidney transplant recipient.

Once the weight of my corporate job was off my back, I set out to really focus on my wellness business. In the beginning, I was a mind-body coach because I've learned that the mind and body are intricately interwoven. I want more people to understand this, so it seemed like a good place to start. After many business courses, I learned that I needed to niche down, so I decided to help corporate executives manage stress. Since I spent most of my working life in the corporate world, I have inside experience to help this group of people. My business coach helped me hone in on my messaging, and in September 2024, I launched my wellness program, which was also a fearful experience, but she guided me through it.

More recently, however, I had a realization that my messaging felt dull, masculine, and corporate. I needed a change because if I didn't feel good about my own message and if it didn't make my own heart quicken and my own spirit rise, how could my potential clients possibly feel the spark of connection and possibility? Again, with the help of my coach, I decided to help organ transplant recipients live a healthy life using holistic remedies that complement allopathic medicine. This feels good because it's where I began my wellness journey.

My transplant wasn't just a medical procedure noted in a hospital chart; it was the beginning of a spiritual journey that continues to unfold with each mindful choice I make about my well-being.

What all of these experiences have taught me is that I can live life to the fullest as long as I don't let fear creep in. As I continue down this road of life, I intend to do that which scares me, create new experiences, and reinvent myself as often as possible. I hope that you will learn from my stories and create a life you love, no matter your age.

Tammy Cameron

Calm Strategy
Holistic Educator

https://www.facebook.com/Calm.Strategy
https://www.instagram.com/tammystma/
https://calmstrategy.ca/

Tammy is a compassionate educator with a passion for reading, writing, and all forms of sharing stories. The stories she writes are stories of courage and connection that engage the reader with new perspectives and a process of inner reflection. Tammy draws on over 25 years of experience in facilitated classroom, boardroom, and conference room adult education and staff training. She has taught at colleges and universities across North America. She delivers practical strategies for developing calm spaces were productivity and creativity shine. Having faced significant health challenges at a young age, she knows struggle and resilience. She has cried intensely over a dropped grape, focused profoundly on breathing to get through extreme physical pain, and has climbed a mountain in high-heeled sandals because she could! She most often writes in the early morning, alongside the sunrise, with a view of pine trees and basswood dancing in a gentle breeze.

The Ember Within

By Tammy Cameron

As a young girl, I was enthralled by documentaries. I loved life stories from around the world. I was fascinated with the resourcefulness of humans, and I was always curious about the lives of others. One documentary stuck in my memory like glue. A young mother of two small children, aged under four, was married and lived in a remote village in Africa. I have forgotten the name of the village; I have never forgotten the woman's story. Her husband had a long daily walk to get to his job, two hours each way. To have strength for the walk, he needed calories. The four-year-old needed calories for his growing bones and muscles, and the one-year-old similarly needed calories for her development, yet the mother's milk had dried up due to a lack of nourishment for herself. Daily, the family had one seed. With care, the woman crushed that seed. Then, she added water and mixed the crushed seed to make a paste. The husband ate first. With the tiny portion that remained in the bowl following the husband's meal, the woman again added water, mixing carefully, not spilling a drop. She fed her two children, and finally, she drank herself.

I wanted to be like this woman. That sounds surprising, I know. My desire was not to live in another country, nor was it to be married or to have two children. My desire certainly was not to live in a state of lack or struggle. My desire was deeper than all these observations. I desired to engage in my environment and take deliberate action with care, so that those around me may benefit. I desired to make the most of my moments. I desired to miraculously create something amazing out of something simple, and to me, a meal for four from one seed was an example of this exact transformation.

You can also transform your current situation, in any area of your life, into something amazing from exactly where you are right now. That is, if it is something that you want to do. You deserve the best moments.

I have been told it is my gift to see others, to know them deeply, and to understand their motivations and worries from brief interactions. That is how I know your greatness. If you were drawn to this book, heard the message spoken by the cover image, courageously opened the pages, began reading, and found your way to this chapter and this page, you have indisputable greatness within you.

Think of some ways that greatness appears in the world: the birth of a baby, the metamorphosis from caterpillar to butterfly, the formation of magma into granite, and countless natural wonders. One moment, there's incubation, and the next, there's revelation. Give yourself permission to incubate and to emerge from your metamorphosis. Change takes effort and time. It might be messy. It requires patience. It takes thought. Permission begins with you.

During and following university, I experienced enormous challenges with my health. Mysterious pain came that could not be explained, and it continued to plague me for eleven and a half months. When the issue was finally discovered and resolved, recovery was a difficult journey, one that taxed and depleted my energy and tired my spirit. Nevertheless, I was determined to live my best moments. I gave myself permission to grieve, to rest, to express frustration and despair, to make continued but small efforts to do more each day. Seeing my desperation in select moments, my doctor would tell me, "If you can't do something for your body, do something for your mind." Already an avid reader, I allowed myself to read more. I engaged in deep solitude with my own breath as a strategy to move through physical pain. And more than anything, I engaged with my creative self, finding new ways to manage day-to-day activities: clutching pillows tightly to my cut muscles so I could enjoy laughing at a joke, laying on my side on the sofa with one leg propped up at an odd angle, and one arm hanging over the side so my brother could beat me yet again at chess on a fabric board with light pieces that I could sometimes move or sometimes direct him to move for me when I could not manage the exertion to reach. I learned to wrap my feet in T-shirts for warmth because bending in any way to put on socks was impossible, and some days, I was too stubborn to accept help with this task. More of this story is shared in the anthology *She Stands Strong: 30 Personal Stories of Strength and Resilience.* It was during this part of my life story that I birthed the person I am today. I had my seed. I was breathing. I resolved to make the most of my best moments. It started with giving myself permission to be afraid, upset, confused, worried, confident, determined, persistent, grateful, and ready to fight for my next chapter.

Some life stages are more peaceful than others, and gratefully, I experienced those: travel, friendship, work-life balance, family, career, and all the good that comes along with these adventures. Our greatest personal accomplishments, though, and our proudest moments, seem to be birthed from the more chaotic and challenging times.

In my early thirties, I thought that I had some parts of life figured out well. I was independent, educated, employed, and dating, and times were good. A new significant other entered the scene, and this is where things went very, very wrong. Women tend to compromise a lot; it begins small, until finally, we have compromised so much that parts of ourselves are gone, missing, and somewhat forgotten. It started out well. I blinked, and my life had turned into a bad movie. Eventually, I was the lead character standing there, observing, almost not believing, and wondering where it went wrong and where I was when it happened. I had compromised so much to make another person happy that I was no longer the me that I knew. This story can become quite long itself, and I have discovered over the years that we can learn without reliving and retelling things over again. I will share with you the reality that came to be: my home became full of "stuff"—from collectibles to art to movies to a full-size, two-person arcade game in the middle of my living room, delivered and placed while I was at work against my wishes. I was woken up one night (a weeknight and a worknight) shortly after 11 p.m., to be asked to smell the new "Dragon Knight" cologne and to offer my opinion on whether I thought it would be good for a "first date" with another woman. I was introduced to a "new girlfriend" (not the woman from the previously mentioned date) in my own home and was introduced as "just a friend" after being together for four years. A new car was purchased for the purpose of "cruising for women." Repeated requests for this now ex-partner to move out were ignored as he believed the living arrangement was "great." When my tolerance reached its limit, I moved. This was the final scene of this chapter. Again, with much relief, I birthed my new self. I left my destructive environment deliberately and with care, bringing peace back into my world and into the world of those around me. It started with giving myself permission to no longer wait for the change that I needed, to forgive the voices of my family urging me to act faster when I wasn't capable, to make efforts to part amicably in spite of wrongdoings, to allow myself to gently rediscover my own interests and hobbies, and to allow big, open windows of time for reflecting, star-gazing, and listening to silence.

Again, I was drawn into some peaceful moments, productive years, and happy times. I sailed happily through this life phase and considered myself to be blessed. All was good until it suddenly was not. I got a new boss. This experience was like no other, and I endured a difficult year trying to navigate this relationship. I was hopeful. I put in every effort. I answered all questions and shared every piece of knowledge and expertise I had to offer. I was pulled away from projects that I had once championed and from professional relationships that I had initiated and nurtured over time. I was disconnected from cherished colleagues. This new relationship somehow did not work out. My position was fully eliminated under this new leadership, and my feelings were mixed.

After years of loyal service and demonstrated dedication at a job with a purpose that fueled my heart, my daily world changed in an instant. Nevertheless, it is these exact experiences that bring the birth of something new and amazing. This part of my story is still unfolding. As I breathe into it, I allow myself permission to recognize my value, to accept kind words and earned compliments from others, to become excited about new possibilities, to collaborate with like-minded individuals and organizations, and to build a new professional family. I have my seed. I am practiced at taking deliberate action with care. Something simple sits before me—a new, blank canvas. Now is my time to incubate until the miraculous, next step is ready to unfold and reveal itself.

How long have you stayed in an unfulfilling relationship, job, or geographical location? How many compromises have you made that do not feel good to your core self? Are you acting and making decisions to please yourself or to please others? Are you responding to your soul's desires? Your answers are all okay. Please read that sentence again. Your answers are all okay. I had a teacher in my holistic training program who always told us that a successful result for our client depends on finding the right treatment for the right set of personal circumstances at the right time. Only you know your exact needs, actions, and timing. Others can guide you, encourage you, and even pressure you, but only you can best recognize how and when to act. Trust yourself.

If I am to guide you here, I will tell you that you know your value. You know your timing. You deserve rest, and you deserve action. You deserve support. You deserve to be seen and heard. You deserve to experience and share your best moments with yourself, your family, your community, and the world. Give yourself full permission to shine your light. I recall reading an anecdote many years ago. Henry Ford had been interviewed and was asked about designing and building products that his customers would want. He replied that if he asked his customers what they wanted, they would tell him that they wanted a faster horse. The world does not know what you have to offer until you show up and demonstrate. Life is too short to simply sit at the side of the pool. Jump in! Bring your best to the party.

What permissions have you been denying yourself? Do not worry about the reasons why. Instead, ask yourself how you can allow yourself what you need. Some of my permissions to myself are authenticity of emotion, forgiveness, self-care, acceptance, collaboration, and anticipation of new possibilities. Your permissions may be entirely different than my examples, and they will be perfect for you. Identify. Allow. Act in harmony.

Like the woman in the documentary from my childhood crushed her seed, with the same care, identify your core desire. What makes your heart sing, your creativity flow, and your core self feel whole? This is part of your unique, inner self.

As she added the water, not spilling a drop to make her paste, you add your self-permissions, fully cherished, without filter or omission. What have you been denying yourself? Can you now allow it?

As she nourished her family and drank herself, share your strength, power, knowledge, and creation with those around you, and in doing so, feed your own soul. What can you begin, even on a small scale, that makes a positive impact on something or someone in your environment?

Take deliberate action with care. Make the best of your moments. See the miraculous possibility in simplicity.

Transformation itself is not a glamorous process, but it is gloriously rewarding. The glamour comes at the end, after you have done the work, put in the effort, and consistently shown up for yourself. In society magazines and social media posts, we see the result of transformation: celebration, achievement, success, and big smiles. We do not see the full process of what it took to get there.

Along the journey of transformation, we find ordinary people living their lives, managing the circumstances that come their way, living through times of heartache, hardship, and even moments of regret, because this is our collective human experience. As we navigate and balance challenging times with days of ease, we discover empowering practices like self-care, setting boundaries, prioritizing goals, and overcoming discouragement. Through all of this, we learn, and we come to know ourselves deeply. Within is the light, the energetic ember waiting to emerge. Nourish it. Care for it. Shower it with love and consideration. And when your ember sparks, feed it. Listen to your soul's desire. Honour the flame and let the fire burn. Dance, discover, unveil, and fully unleash this power within. Claim who you are. Your potential is limitless.

For how long have you fenced yourself in with limitations? How much longer do you want to wait? Let yourself live large and free. Give yourself permission.

The miracle is the process of making paste from a seed. It is the comfort after an extended period of pain, the peace after a challenging relationship, and the recovery after the loss of something or someone cherished. What is the miracle for you today? What do you want to create in your world?

As much as I loved documentaries as a child, I also watched cartoons. I learned the power of laughter, silliness, creative problem-solving, and bold expression of personality. I learned acceptance, tolerance of differences, and teamwork. I want more of this in my world. As I embark on my next chapter, I resolve to nurture this ember within, to bring it into my community in greater ways, and to let the art on my blank canvas begin to form. I give myself permission to provide the time needed to engage daily in happy thoughts and fun activities. I find ways to remind myself of the importance of play. I know my value. My potential is expansive. I bring benefit to those around me through deliberate action with care. I make the most of my moments. I miraculously create something amazing from something simple. I learn, grow, and transform into the newest version of myself yet.

My wish for you is that you remain always curious, with an open heart, and eager to learn. May you allow yourself permission to spark and nurture your personal ember within; may its voice remain steady, strong, and clear. Stand up, smile, and sing your song. Unleash your unique lyrics. No one sings like you. The theme is yours to choose. You cannot be out of tune with your own music! Transform your seed into nourishing paste. You deserve the miracle. From exactly where you are right now, grant yourself permission to proceed and create something amazing!

Carmen Maendel

Nate's Property Maintenance LLC
Co-Owner/Business Office Manager

https://www.linkedin.com/in/carmen-maendel-17510944/
https://www.facebook.com/ncmaendel
https://www.instagram.com/maendelcarmen/
http://natespropertymaintenance.com

Hello I'm Carmen Maendel. Nate and I are a husband and wife team. Our fifteen year old son, Josh officially works for our company as well. We have embarked upon an entrepreneurial journey together that is extremely rewarding for all of us. We own and operate Nate's Property Maintenance LLC together. I handle the business on the home front while my husband coordinates our projects on the job sites with our clients and team of workers. We compliment each other very well working together, and remain very service oriented in our company. Some of the business roles I perform are the following: balancing our books, regularly posting to social media, scheduling our clients, arranging purchase contracts for new business equipment, keeping our business licenses and registration up to date, documenting client files, and much more. Nate works with our clients by coordinating all the projects and equipment on the job sites and carefully plans for each of our projects we do down to the finest of details. Nate, Josh, and Carmen

With the Helmet of Salvation

By Carmen Maendel

Introduction: I Am a Child of God

Hello, friend, I am Carmen Maendel, and I am a child of God, a mother, and a wife. I came to the Lord at the early age of thirteen; however, I rededicated my life to Christ as an adult on November 4, 2006. This does not mean that I am perfect or have not had adversity in my life. Quite the opposite, I would say. Some of the negative incidents in my life happen when I am seeking the Lord wholeheartedly. In this book, *Unleash Her: The Next Chapter Begins*, in my chapter "With the Helmet of Salvation," I will share some life-altering moments with you about how I was saved and how I wear my "Helmet of Salvation" on a daily basis. My narrative begins prior to my rededication to Christ, with a traumatic event that God used for His Glory to help me train over fifty women in our Maendel Fitness Gym & Spa several years later.

Grocery Store Incident: Creepy Men Stalking Me

It was a normal day for me, working as a Stockbroker and Financial Advisor at that time. I have always aimed at maintaining a specific structure in my life, and to this day develop daily routines and systems that help my day run more smoothly and productively. I left the office and headed to a commercial gym to work out. I had just invested in a lifetime membership with this gym and felt pretty good about putting all this in place to increase my likelihood of staying invested in my workouts. I finished my workout and began to walk to my car to go home that evening. I knew the grocery store was right behind the gym, so I stopped off to grab a few items on the way home. This is where the nightmare began. I was standing in the check-out lane, and a guy from the gym, who taught self-defense, was standing right behind me. He told me, "There are three men who have been following you in this store." I had an immediate choice to make in whether I was going to trust and believe him, or think that he may have some part in all this, too. He asked me, "Would you like me to walk you to your car tonight?" I decided that a friendly face from the gym was more inviting than having three men tailing me out to my car.

As we walked out to my car, I noticed that the three men that he told me about had parked immediately across from my JAG and were slinking way down in their seats, watching me. They wore blue jeans and down orange colored vests that night. I asked the guy that was walking me to my car to please stay with me, as my heart was beginning to race, and I had determined that these three men were definitely up to no good. He proceeded to help me put my groceries in the car and then sat down in the driver's seat as I got into the passenger seat. He started my car and pulled it around to the back of the store, and we called the police immediately. The police came, but those three men took off long before they even got there. Tags were spotted on their vehicle, and it turned out they were from some country town outside of Colorado Springs, CO. I remember being very afraid that night to go back alone to my apartment. I called up a friend of mine and they came over immediately and stayed that night to make sure I was alright. It is amazing how violated I felt even when none of them touched me. It was the fear of what might have happened that encouraged me to take steps of empowerment toward being able to defend myself in any given scenario. To this day, I am very vigilant to pay attention to anyone who seems like they are following me. The next day, I enrolled in a Russian self-defense class and learned some techniques that would help defend myself if anything like this were to happen again in my life. I didn't even know God to the extent that I do today, and He protected me that evening by placing that man behind me in the grocery store. This incident, coupled with the next event I will share with you, is what helped fuel my desire and passion to build a gym in our home today.

The Other Half of the Equation: My Father's Battle with Cancer

The other half of the equation for building the gym in our home came from the experience of my dad going into a state of unresponsiveness with his cancer. He fought long and hard for his life for about fifteen years. Coming from a medical background, he was able to try all the innovative medical technology and unique treatments for cancer. What had started out as prostate cancer had moved into other areas of his body and metastasized to the bone. By this time, his doctor described his cancer as throwing seeds into a field, and they just grew and grew at that point without ceasing. He became unresponsive at the later stages of his cancer, which finally spread to his brain. He was an orthopedic surgeon and understood what was happening to him. He was very aggravated and seemed to understand medically what was happening to him, yet he had no control over it. I vowed to myself that night that I would get myself into the best possible physical condition I could and maintain that throughout my lifetime. Cancer runs on my father's side of the family, and we have lost several family members to it. Diabetes and strokes run on my mother's side, too, so I figured I would get myself into top physical condition and stay there for life in case something ever happened to me. I am glad I did because I did encounter several more medical challenges in my life that I will talk about in this chapter as well.

Passion for Health and Fitness: HHFM Ministry and Maendel Fitness

I knew after my terrifying experience of being stalked that I would never want to belong to a commercial gym again. I have always had a passion for health and fitness, so the only logical solution seemed to be creating our own gym space in the basement of the home my husband and I purchased here in Minnesota. I started purchasing a few items for the gym and began working out myself regularly in our basement gym. I felt guilty that this big, beautiful gym space was being used solely by me. I started inviting friends over one by one to come work out with me in our gym. This led to me officially starting HHFM Heritage Health and Fitness Ministry at our church at that time. We had five or six ladies come together to work out regularly, once or twice a week. It was an amazing fellowship and an incredible way God used for me to begin to connect with women and exercise in a deep and meaningful way. I remember having about five Schwinn Airdyne bikes and doing HIIT High Intensity Interval Training workouts and cycling classes with them. We even had a room connected, dedicated to childcare, for the women working out in our gym. I led this ministry for about four years prior to deciding to attain my certificate as a Certified Fitness Trainer in 2016. This was the same year that I founded Maendel Fitness and started working with fitness clients in our basement gym. I realized that it was important to combine both fitness and nutrition, so I also got my master's degree in Nutrition and DNA Testing a few years later. God helped me work with my clients and achieve major breakthroughs in their lives that went way beyond just losing weight on a scale.

Vibrant You: Elevating Your Self-Confidence with Affirmations and Self-Love

Some of the things I worked on with my clients helped them elevate their confidence with affirmations and self-love. I asked them to pick a verse in the Bible that they believed in and could stand strong with. We also worked on affirmations and "I Can" statements to help reinforce their confidence in the things they could do and deflected those things that they could not do. I taught them that every obstacle that they face offers an opportunity to improve. I encouraged them to view adversity in their lives as opportunities with solutions, rather than problems and stumbling blocks. Pushing through challenging moments in your life will help you reach a higher level. It may take us a while to accomplish something in life, but eventually we will succeed if we keep on trying. According to Burton Kanter, "You miss one hundred percent of the shots you don't take." You need to just keep swinging and not give up! "You can't hit the ball (get a hit) if you don't swing (the bat)," said Wayne Gretzky. The definition of self-confidence is the feeling of trust in one's abilities, qualities, and judgment. What if you are a person who suffers from low self-esteem and lacks self-confidence? I have good news for you! Self-confidence is a skill. Self-confidence is something that we can all learn to master, given lots of practice and perseverance. Whatever that thing is that you feel weak at, spend more time on that than any other activity, and you will improve over time. Self-confidence is an attitude about your skills and abilities. It means you accept and trust yourself and God, and have a sense of control in your life. You know your strengths and weaknesses very well, yet you still have a positive view of yourself.

Keys to Self-Confidence

- Recognize what you excel at
- Build positive relationships
- Be kind to yourself
- Learn to be assertive
- Learn to say "no"
- Give yourself challenges
- Surround yourself with positive people
- Take care of your body
- Practice positive self-talk
- Face your fears
- Be in competition with only yourself
- Stop comparing yourself to others

Four Areas This Can Have a Positive Effect on Our Lives

1) Better performance at work or in the home:

You don't waste time worrying that you are not good enough. Instead, you can devote all your energy to your efforts, which lead to better performance.

2) Healthy relationships:

It impacts how you feel about yourself, and it helps you better understand and love others. It also gives us the strength to walk away if we are not being treated well.

3) Openness to try new things:

When you believe in yourself, you will be open to trying new things.

4) Resilience:

Believing in yourself can enhance your resilience and ability to recover from any challenges or adversities you face in life.

Keys to Affirmation

- Words that lift you and others up
- Positive words about self or others
- Feel good words
- Emotional support words
- Encouraging words

Self-Affirmations

- I am worth all the love I receive
- I am a beautiful creation
- I can handle all the challenges that I encounter
- I can do great things
- I am going to be successful
- I will not let failures get the best of me

More Positive Affirmations

- I have a purpose and was created with divine intention
- I can and I will...end of story
- I overcome my fears by meeting them head-on
- I feed my spirit and feed my body at the same time
- I am in charge of my own life through the decisions I make
- I will not compare myself to others in person or on the internet
- I am choosing and doing instead of sitting and wishing
- I am worthy and enough
- I am loved and cherished
- I have the power, within myself, to create change
- I believe good things are coming into my life
- I am strong and can get through anything in life with God by my side
- I will accomplish all that I set out to conquer in life with God's strength and not my own
- I request my desires, through prayer, and I am ready to receive them all
- I am going to make you so proud of me
- I am powerful and strong
- I am truly unstoppable
- I go after what I want and I get it when it aligns with God's will for my life
- My mind, body, and soul are super healthy
- I forgive those who have harmed me in the past
- I am the architect of my own life, and God directs my steps

Story: The Architect

I want to share a story with you that I also shared with my fitness and nutrition clients about their lives. So, there once was a man who was an incredible architect. Whenever there was an extremely challenging project, this architect was brought on to lead the project. For many years, he built the most amazing buildings and structures around. He was even called in from out of state for specific, intricate building projects as well. After doing this for over thirty years, he came to his boss and told him, "I think this will be my final project as I am looking to move into other areas of my life right now." His boss was very sorry to see him go, however, he had deep respect for him and understood why he wanted to leave the firm. His boss asked him, "I have one final project I would love for you to do for me, and then you are free to go." So, the man set out to complete his final project. Materials were scarce and very expensive, so he found himself cutting corners on this project like he had never even considered doing on his former projects throughout the years. He raced through this one without doing his best work. He mostly just cared about finishing it and being done with it. Finally, the project was completed, and he walked into his boss's office to tell him that he was done. His boss gave him a hug and thanked him for all the long, hard years he had put into this firm. He then said, "Here, I want you to have the keys to this home you just created; it is my gift to you." Suddenly, the architect felt a sick feeling in his stomach. Had he known his boss was going to give him this home, he would have put much more effort into this project. He would have used much nicer material and not cut corners on the quality of craftsmanship involved in building this home. Did you know that the average person puts more thought into planning a vacation than into the details of living their life? Don't make the same mistake that this architect did. Make sure you plan carefully the details of your life. "We may make our plans, but the Lord determines our steps" (Proverbs 16:9).

Building Maendel Fitness: Adversity and Obstacles Along the Way

I can recall four major setbacks that happened as I was building the gym and training clients over the eight-year period that I did. The first setback was the storm damage that happened to our gym. I remember laying down towels on the basement floor, and they would be soaked in an hour. I remember standing in the gym with tears rolling down my face, my friend hugging me and reassuring me that everything would be alright. We did two full remodels in the gym, only to have the same problem happen again. This happened on two occasions in the spring, and the last time it happened, we decided to invest in very expensive drain tile around our gym and basement to save my company, Maendel Fitness. We also invested in a triple-safe sump pump system. I remember continuing to train my annual clients upstairs in our living-entertainment room, which served as a makeshift gym for about three months while they were repairing the gym. If I had thrown in the towel, I would never have seen the plans God had for us to expand our gym into a spa and sauna area and a seven-person Jacuzzi out back.

The next setback was that I had injured my back earlier in life and re-injured it while I was swinging on a hammock that Nate and I had brought back from Mexico. I was swinging very high on his hammock, and our son, Josh, was watching me. All of a sudden, the hammock snapped and I went flying to the ground. I had numerous issues with my back after that, and I even looked at back surgery as a solution to my problem. We realized that the bed we were sleeping on did not have the excellent back support that I needed; it had a broken board underneath. We replaced the board, and slowly, I began to heal again. I remember my sister-in-law sold me their tread climber, which their family had bought some time ago and never used. I used this machine to help strengthen my core, along with specific core exercises, without putting any pressure on my back. The core and the back work together, so if you have a weak core, you automatically also have a weak back. To this day, I make sure to have a very strong core and back so that I am less susceptible to back injuries in the future.

The next setback was right before we did our grand reopening of Maendel Fitness after it had been remodeled for the second time. I was in the gym with my friend and her daughter. I had done an intensive hour-long kickboxing workout before they even got there. We started working out on the gym equipment, doing a cardio HIIT circuit training workout. I remember I was working out on the rowing machine, and all of a sudden, I told my friend, "I have had enough." She was surprised because usually she called me the Energizer Bunny when it came to working out. Her daughter then spilled some water on the gym floor. Because of our past history with water in the gym, I freaked out and jumped up to find a towel to clean it up. I ran into the laundry room right next door and luckily found a towel. If I had run upstairs, there is a chance that I might have fallen down those stairs unconscious. What happened next, I asked my friend to tell me, as I was unconscious myself.

Apparently, after grabbing the towel, I came into the gym and was standing holding the corner of the wooden beam. I fell directly backwards, hitting my head on the Airdyne bike peg. If the peg had not been there, I would have fallen directly on the back of my head on the concrete floor. God protected me from this happening. I was knocked out for a few moments, and my friend told me that my body went into convulsions. I came to and realized that blood was streaming down the back of my neck. My friend took me immediately into the ER with a towel wrapped tightly around my head. As we were driving there, I was worried that I had suffered memory loss, so I kept asking her questions that she would know the answer to. She finally said to me, "Carmen, if you are asking me these questions, then you clearly don't have memory loss." We got to the hospital, and my husband greeted me with a rubber plant and a beautiful card. The doctor put seven staples in the back of my head that day. My doctor suspected that my blood pressure dropped because I did not eat enough that day, and I was drinking tea with Stevia in it. I have a very low athletic blood pressure anyway, and Stevia may have lowered it to an unsafe level and caused me to pass out.

I was afraid to work out in the gym that I had created, listening to God guide me along the way. This was a bit ironic. I was a fitness and nutrition trainer who was afraid to work out alone in our gym. I continued to train fitness and nutrition clients in our gym and kept this incident very quiet at that time, so none of my clients knew about it. I slowly built up my confidence to work out alone in our gym again. I began by making sure I always have my phone with me in the gym so that if something ever happened, I could get help. I started with very short workouts just to prove to myself that I can do this. I eventually made them into longer workouts and started training regularly in our gym again. I knew if I did not "get back up on the horse" again after being bucked off, that I never would. Still to this day, I get up at 5:50 a.m. for my workout so that I can complete it before my son and husband leave our home, and I always take my phone with me to the gym.

This brings me to the final incident that occurred while owning Maendel Fitness. The winter of 2021 was a very difficult time for all of us. We had lost my husband's brother earlier that year, and Nate's dad, who I was super close to, passed away on December 8, 2021. I was able to have one final conversation with his dad on the phone the morning before he passed away; however, I had a serious case of COVID-19 pneumonia, so I was not able to go with my family to the hospital to say goodbye. For the entire month of December into January, I was laid up on the sofa in our family room. I remember sitting on the edge of our bed, gasping for air with the bedroom window open. I was the sickest I have ever been in my entire life and probably should have gone to the hospital. I stuck it out at home, and our son stayed home from school to take care of me while Nate was working outside our home. Our son, Josh, would make me soup, different dishes, and my green smoothies to help me regain my strength. I literally could not stand up for a while to make a meal. Our church family was very kind and brought in a variety of meals for all of us during that time. I remember setting the timer on the hour, so that I would go out to our landing in the garage and practice breathing for one minute. I would take a deep inhale and then slowly exhale the air. I would repeat this process for about one minute. My brother-in-law knew quite a bit about health and sickness, so he brought me a concoction of pills and liquids that truly did help me get better. I will always remember that period of time when our gym was shut down completely by our Minnesota governor during COVID, and God had some big plans for the gym shortly after that time.

Story: Three Feet from Gold (Napoleon Hill, *Think and Grow Rich*)

I have one final story for you that I hope serves as encouragement to you. There was once a man who was very dedicated to finding gold out west. He had moved his family out there, and they panned for gold every single day for twenty years. He found small hints of gold but never found anything extremely valuable. One day he told his wife, "That's it, I'm done!" He had spent all that time looking for gold and never found it, and he was throwing in the towel. He packed up his family and left the next day. That same day, a young, energetic gold miner showed up to take over his spot for mining gold. He moved over just a little bit and struck gold that day. The first miner was three feet from striking gold, and he gave up. If he had had a little more staying power and discipline, he might have been the one who struck gold that day. Never, never, never give up! Your destination or goal may be closer than you think, and you will never know because you gave up! "Keep on swingin'...don't ever stop!"

RESOURCES:

Maendel Fitness & Nutrition Resources

Carmen Maendel YouTube Channel
https://www.youtube.com/@carmenmaendel6186

MFC Muscle Menu
https://drive.google.com/file/d/1iob0qnW2TLD8CE7cj9gLx9jP8hG
1Jcfn/view?usp=sharing

MFC Guru Grocery List
https://drive.google.com/file/d/1FHt77_tiJostf7lEKNYzbeYTEqAG7i
1L/view?usp=sharing

MFC Tasty & Savory Cookbook
https://drive.google.com/file/d/1RItKdZqlntip1Bh7AEzC67020xQm
rJ_k/view?usp=sharing

MFC Confidence Boost System
https://drive.google.com/file/d/1wo7usMTuOzO1y3YHEglm-
r7wnAydP7cv/view?usp=sharing

MFC I Can Statements Worksheet
https://drive.google.com/file/d/1oSLTWLCWLpdw6xQEWBIkd9D3
IfBCSpG3/view?usp=sharing

Kim Rendon

The Menopause Rebel
Registered Dietitian, Health Coach

https://www.linkedin.com/in/kimrendon/
https://www.facebook.com/kim.rendon.31392
https://www.instagram.com/the.menopause.rebel/
https://menopause-rebel.com/
https://www.youtube.com/@themenopauserebel

Kim Rendon brings 32 years of experience as a registered dietitian to her work, but it's her personal journey of transformation that truly fuels her passion. After balancing a demanding career while being a wife and raising two active boys, Kim discovered her own path to vibrant health and now guides women navigating life's transformative transitions. As a certified health coach, gut health specialist, and hormone health expert, she combines evidence-based knowledge with real-world wisdom. Through her work as The Menopause Rebel, Kim champions the revolutionary idea that women get to do menopause their way, breaking free from outdated expectations. Her approach blends practical nutrition guidance with deep compassion, helping women reclaim their power during significant life changes. When not empowering others, you'll find Kim in her happy place—soaking up sunshine at the beach, embodying the freedom and joy she helps her clients discover within themselves.

Rediscovering Myself

By Kim Rendon

Have you ever had a time when enough is enough? Yeah, I did. It was the summer of 2021, and I decided I was tired of feeling tired, tired of the depression, and tired of dragging myself through each day.

But let's take a step back to how I got to this point.

I was the mom who worked full-time, the mom who couldn't say no to all the activities at school and church. (Because if they couldn't find anyone else, how would it get done?) I was the wife who got up early to make lunch for her husband and made sure he had dinner ready when he got home, even if I had places to be after work. I was the woman who didn't take time for herself. My life was so centered around my family that I didn't even think about myself.

Through those years, I struggled on and off with depression and would sometimes use antidepressants to help manage the symptoms. In June 2018, my oldest son left home to join the Marine Corps. About seven months later, my husband moved out.

The depression hit hard, and I tend to eat my feelings. Cookies, cakes, brownies, ice cream, you get the idea—anything sweet. I gained the weight I had worked so hard to lose, and then gained some more. This made the depression worse because I was mad at myself for gaining all the weight. I even said to myself a couple of times that I hated myself.

In the fall of 2019, my youngest started his senior year, and all the "lasts" were marked off. The last first football game of the season, the last last game of the season, the last first wrestling meet. You get it, right? I began to feel like I was losing my sense of identity. Who will I be now?

And then 2020 happened. I was working at the health department, and we were responsible for giving out the vaccines. Those were long and stressful days that had me running on empty.

Then, it all hit me all at once. I felt like I couldn't go on. I wanted out of my job, but I didn't know what I would do. And that's when I hit my breaking point.

I took a leave from work and tried to figure out where to go from there. I was an emotional mess, overwhelmed, and honestly, I didn't know who I was anymore. I was no longer the boy mom, the team mom, the booster VP, or the wife.

In the beginning, I took time each day for prayer and meditation, learning to listen to my body and what it needed. I spent a lot of time sitting on the beach, soaking up the sun, getting my feet into the sand, and crying. Then, I remembered having a Craniosacral Therapy (CST) session one time. CST is used to help release both emotional and physical stress, which would be a good place to start my healing journey. It just happened that the naturopathic practitioner who did the CST specialized in Nutrition Response Testing (NRT). This complementary healing approach identifies nutritional imbalances and weaknesses in the body's systems, then uses targeted nutritional support to help the body heal itself.

I decided that NRT would be the next step in my healing journey. After my initial analysis, she identified adrenal exhaustion from being too stressed (Hmm, ya think?) and issues with my thyroid.

Through the NRT, I began to change my diet. I started by writing down everything I ate. Then, she had me eliminate sugar, not just the added sugar, but also reading labels and finding where it was hidden in my food. Have you ever looked at how much sugar is in the food you eat? I needed to make sure my meals contained a fiber, a protein, and a fat. As a dietitian who went to college in the 80s, adding fat to my diet was scary. However, it's not just any fat, but a healthy fat like avocados, avocado oil, coconut oil, olive oil, or nuts and seeds. Our bodies require these healthy fats for many important functions.

Next up, healing my gut. Why my gut, you may ask. Our gut is the root of many medical conditions and illnesses we have. There is a connection between the brain and the gut. It affects our immunity and is linked to autoimmune issues, cardiac health, bone health, hormones, and even our perimenopause/menopause symptoms. Ninety percent of our serotonin is produced in our gut.

Essential oils and products containing them have become another important part of my routine. By using these natural alternatives, I've eliminated many toxins I would have been exposed to through synthetic products. These oils support me in multiple ways—they help balance my emotions and manage my mood, create either calming or uplifting environments depending on what I need, and strengthen my body's natural immune function.

About a year later, I began working with the Emotion Code and Body Code healing modalities. These techniques identify and release trapped energies and unprocessed emotions that often contribute to both physical health issues and mental conditions we experience.

Then, I discovered Biofield Tuning, a healing method that uses sound vibrations to help release stuck energy and restore balance in the body. It works by clearing out the emotional and physical traumas stored in our energy field, helping both the body and mind heal on a deeper level. I've been using this technique for the past year.

Lastly, I have added talk therapy. I have been coordinating my Biofied Tunings and therapy sessions. Talking with my therapist a day or two after a tuning session helps me process what has come up during the tuning session. One of the times I was talking with my therapist, she told me that by doing this deeper energetic healing, I was farther ahead of others that she works with. She would have been able to go only so far with the talk therapy. Talk therapy addresses what we consciously know. It can only go so far in uncovering the deeper, subconscious beliefs and emotions rooted in past hurts and traumas—things that energy work can help release and heal.

We all go through things in life—sometimes big, sometimes small— that affect how we handle our emotions. The stuff we bury (I like to call it my mental shit) doesn't just go away; it stays in our bodies, causing tension, mood swings, and patterns that hold us back. When we don't fully process and release those emotions, they get stuck, showing up as physical and emotional struggles, and can cause some of our self-sabotaging habits.

Doing the deep inner work and healing is by no means easy. In fact, there have been times that have been really tough, but true transformation happens when you address your body, your mind, and your soul.

By consciously choosing to face and release these trapped energies, we create space for our authentic selves to emerge.

You are probably thinking, "WOW!! That is a lot." While yes, it is; it was done in stages. The Emotion Code/Body Code is only when my body tells me it needs it, and CST happens about twice per year. The Biofield Tuning and visits with my naturopath are done every month. It's important to listen to my body and let it tell me what I need at that moment. You may not need or want to do all of this, but let me tell you why it has worked for me.

First of all, I had to calm my nervous system, which was done through craniosacral therapy. I had been in constant stress mode for so long that my body was basically stuck in fight-or-flight mode. When your body is always on high alert, it's not focused on healing. It's just trying to keep you safe from the next crisis! Getting my body to finally relax and feel safe allowed it to start the healing process.

Next, I focused on getting my physical body back on track through nutrition and healing my gut. Even if you eat the healthiest diet and take all the vitamins and minerals, if your gut isn't healthy or you're in fight-or-flight mode, you won't absorb the nutrients your body needs. Once I cleaned up my diet by cutting out sugar and giving my body real nourishment, I started to feel my energy coming back. I needed this physical foundation before I could handle the emotional stuff. It's hard to process deep emotions when your body is just trying to survive day to day.

Only after establishing this physical foundation could I address the deeper energetic blocks and trapped emotions that had accumulated over the years. These clearing practices opened channels that had been blocked, allowing energy to flow more freely.

Finally, integrating these shifts through both energy work and conscious processing allowed the healing to become part of my lived experience, not just a temporary relief.

Transformation involves deep healing—physically, emotionally, and spiritually. It's about connecting to your body in new ways, finding balance, and addressing any lingering traumas or imbalances that have been carried through the years. While I did not plan on any of these methods, other than the craniosacral therapy, they all presented themselves at the right time in my journey. Learning to listen to my body when it told me it needed that specific modality. And it was important for my body to do the work in the order it was done.

While this journey was uniquely mine, these steps follow natural patterns that can benefit anyone seeking transformation. You might be drawn to different healing modalities than I was, and that's okay. You get to do what works for you. Here's an overview of approaches that support transformation at different levels to help you consider what might work for you.

1. **Calming nervous system** - Creates safety for deeper healing to begin

2. **Addressing physical body** - Provides energy and resources needed for healing

3. **Clearing energy blocks** - Releases specific trapped emotions and energy patterns. Some of the techniques used for clearing blocks include:

   - Emotion Code/Body Code - Identifies and releases specific trapped emotions through muscle testing and magnets
   - EFT (Emotional Freedom Technique) - Tapping on meridian points while addressing emotional issues
   - TRE (Tension & Trauma Releasing Exercises) - Uses physical tremoring to release stored tension
   - Somatic experiencing - Gently processes trauma stored in the nervous system
   - EMDR - Uses eye movements to process traumatic memories
   - Breathwork - Various techniques that use breath to move through energy blockages
   - Craniosacral therapy - Subtle bodywork that helps release restrictions
   - Yoga - Poses and practices specifically designed to release energy blocks
   - Self-inquiry and shadow work - Conscious exploration of psychological blocks

4. **Harmonizing energy field** - Balances and integrates the entire energy system. Some forms include:

   - Sound therapy - Uses tuning forks, singing bowls, or other sound vibrations to restore coherence to the field
   - Acupuncture - Works with the body's meridian system to balance energy flow
   - Reiki and energy healing - Practitioners channel universal energy to clear blockages and restore balance
   - Qigong and Tai Chi - Movement practices that help energy flow smoothly through the body

- Crystal healing - Using specific stones to influence the energy field
- Salt baths or time in natural water - Help clear and reset the electromagnetic field
- Grounding practices - Direct connection with the earth helps normalize the body's electrical system
- Chakra balancing - Works with the body's energy centers to harmonize the entire field
- Polarity therapy - Balances the body's positive and negative energy poles
- Meditation focused on energy - Visualization practices that help smooth and balance the field

5. **Processing consciously** - Makes meaning of what emerges and integrates insights

6. **Reconnecting with authentic self** - Discovers identity beyond roles and labels

Starting with body healing can be especially helpful for those who feel physically drained or overwhelmed, as it ensures the body has the resources it needs to support emotional and energetic shifts. However, some people find that doing inner work first can help them identify emotional triggers or blockages that are affecting their physical health. However, this can sometimes feel overwhelming if the body isn't in a balanced state yet. You get to choose what works best for you.

As you consider your transformation journey, remember that it doesn't have to look exactly like mine. What matters is that you begin wherever you are, with whatever calls to you first. The healing approaches I've shared are just some options, but these four simple principles have helped me and my clients, no matter which healing path they choose. Here are four ideas that can help guide you on your path:

No Expectations

Approach your healing journey with open curiosity rather than rigid expectations. When we release our grip on exactly how our transformation "should" unfold, we create space for deeper healing than we might have imagined possible. This isn't about lowering expectations—quite the opposite. It's about expanding beyond the limitations of what your mind can currently envision. The most profound changes often arrive in unexpected forms, teaching us exactly what we need in ways we couldn't have predicted.

Be Here Now

Stay fully present in each moment of your healing journey, allowing you to notice subtle shifts and changes you might otherwise miss. When you're not projecting into the future with expectations or dwelling in the past with regrets, you can actually experience transformation as it happens. This presence allows you to respond to what's unfolding rather than what you fear or hope might happen.

No Judgments

Remove the internal critic that can sabotage your healing. Self-judgment creates resistance that blocks transformation. When you judge your progress, emotions, or reactions, you create tension rather than allowing the natural flow of healing to occur. By practicing non-judgment, you create a compassionate inner environment that makes deeper healing possible.

You Always Know

Trust your intuition and inner wisdom. Societal conditioning often teaches us to look outside ourselves for validation and direction when, in reality, we possess an inner compass that always knows what we truly need. Learning to quiet external voices and listen to your deeper knowledge will guide you to healing approaches right for you at each stage. (Remember the gut health thing? Your gut is your second brain, listen to it.)

The beauty of transformation in midlife is that we've gained enough wisdom to reinvent ourselves consciously. We can choose to embrace new careers, hobbies, relationships, or lifestyles. It's never too late to reinvent yourself, try something new, or pursue something you've always wanted to do but never had the time for. This transformation is about integrating our wisdom into a new version of ourselves, one that is more authentic and empowered.

I don't have it all figured out yet, but do we ever? I'm a continual work in progress, but my depression is gone, and I have more energy. Weight loss happened naturally. I'm working on loving myself more, finding my self-worth, and discovering who Kim is now that she's not just the boy mom and the wife.

Carol Salvadori

Founder of LeadLoud Academy
Empowerment Coach

https://www.linkedin.com/in/leadloudacademy/
https://www.facebook.com/leadloudacademyofficial
https://www.instagram.com/leadloudacademy/
www.leadloudacademy.com

Carol is the visionary founder of LEADLoud Academy, where she champions women to awaken their brilliance and lead with confidence. Drawing from her transformative journey in the corporate world, Carol understands the silent struggles many women face, including playing small and battling self-doubt. These experiences fuelled her passion to flip the script on inadequacy and inspire powerful change. Through her academy, she cultivates tools and environments that encourage professional women to amplify their voices and embrace authenticity. As a contributing author to "UnleashHer Voice" and the upcoming "Nice Girls Finish First," Carol shares her story of overcoming rejection to impact those seeking empowerment. Her mission is to guide women towards unlocking their inner wisdom, leading with purpose in a supportive community. Connect with Carol to explore how you can become the extraordinary leader you're meant to be.

Breaking Boundaries:
My Journey to Empowerment and Self-Discovery

By Carol Salvadori

In the pages of *Unleash Her: The Next Chapter Begins*, we explore the incredible potential women possess to rewrite their narratives and inspire global change. My journey is a testament to this powerful movement—an example of how breaking boundaries and embracing personal strength can lead to profound transformation.

Early Boundaries:
Recognizing and Challenging Societal Norms

From an early age, I was acutely aware of the societal norms dictating a woman's role in the world. These unspoken rules suggested limitation rather than liberation, boundaries rather than boundless potential. Growing up, I was taught to be mindful of tradition and caution—values that, while well-meaning, subtly whispered constraints into my developing dreams and ambitions.

The turning point came during my formative years when I began to question these limitations. Education became my catalyst for change. It opened my eyes to possibilities I had never imagined, encouraging me to think critically and set my own standards. This intellectual awakening was the first step in a long journey towards empowerment, forming the bedrock of my belief that women have the right to define their paths.

Discovering Inner Strength: Stepping Into My Power

The journey to empowerment did not come without its challenges. Like many women, I grappled with self-doubt and the fear of stepping outside prescribed boundaries. The internal battle was often more daunting than external obstacles. However, I discovered a profound truth: the strength to overcome fear and doubt was within me all along.

The turning point occurred during my participation in a leadership program aimed at nurturing women's potential. It was here that I learned to appreciate the power of vulnerability and authenticity. Speaking in front of peers, sharing my vision, and receiving validation became transformative experiences. These moments helped me see that my voice was not just worth hearing—it was necessary.

Actionable Strategies for Growth: Building a Transformative Framework

Understanding that personal growth required more than internal change, I sought practical strategies to guide my journey. Here's how I transformed intention into action:

1. **Cultivating a Vision:** I began by establishing a clear vision—identifying my passions and aligning them with my goals. This vision became the compass guiding my actions and decisions, ensuring that each step moved me closer to realizing my dreams.

2. **Setting Intentional Goals:** Setting achievable, intentional goals was crucial. I broke larger ambitions into smaller, manageable tasks, each contributing to the larger picture. This strategy allowed me to celebrate small victories, maintaining momentum and motivation.

3. **Building Resilience:** Resilience became my ally. I embraced setbacks as learning experiences, moving forward with a mindset that valued growth over perfection. Resilience empowered me to remain steadfast, adapting to change and overcoming obstacles.

4. **Fostering a Supportive Network:** Creating a network of like-minded individuals was instrumental. Whether through mentorship, professional organizations, or supportive friendships, surrounding myself with those who encouraged my potential was pivotal. This network provided guidance, inspiration, and a sense of shared purpose.

5. **Continuous Learning:** Pursuing lifelong learning became a deliberate practice. I sought knowledge through various channels—formal education, workshops, and self-directed study—expanding my skills and perspectives and enriching my personal and professional life.

Real-Life Transformations: Stories of Impact and Inspiration

Throughout my journey, I have been inspired by countless stories of women who have embraced their strength and transformed their lives. These narratives serve as reminders of the collective power women hold and the potential to ignite change within communities and beyond.

One profound story is that of a colleague and friend who, against all odds, championed a cause for gender equality within her organization. Her courage and determination not only shifted organizational policies but also inspired a cultural shift, creating a more inclusive and equitable environment for all employees. Her impact exemplifies the ripple effect of empowered women and spurred me to consider how I, too, could contribute to societal change.

Collective Movement: Joining Forces to Amplify Impact

Empowerment is contagious, and in this communal journey, individual transformations contribute to a broader movement. *Unleash Her* is not just a series of personal stories but a collaborative anthem urging women to rise together and break barriers.

As part of this movement, I dedicate myself to facilitating others' empowerment. Through workshops, coaching, and advocacy, I strive to create spaces where women feel validated and valued. These efforts are part of a larger narrative—an ongoing commitment to fostering environments where women thrive, and communities are transformed by inclusivity and innovation.

The Call to Action: Embrace and Amplify Your Voice

Closing this chapter with a call to action, I invite you, the reader, to reflect on your journey. How can you embrace your voice and rewrite the boundaries that others have set? Here are some suggestions:

1. **Embrace Authenticity:** Be true to yourself. Authenticity is your greatest strength, enabling you to connect genuinely with others and inspire change.

2. **Trust Your Instincts:** Listen to your intuition—it will guide you toward opportunities aligned with your values and aspirations.

3. **Take Bold Actions:** Don't be afraid to step outside your comfort zone. Bold actions are the catalysts for growth and transformation.

4. **Build Supportive Relationships:** Seek and nurture relationships that uplift and encourage you. Together, we are stronger, and our collective wisdom is powerful.

5. **Share Your Story:** Your experiences are valuable, offering guidance and inspiration to those embarking on similar paths. Share your story and illuminate the way for others.

Conclusion: A New Chapter Begins

Reflecting on my journey, I recognize the significance of personal and collective empowerment. Each step taken, each boundary challenged, contributes to a larger, global movement aimed at redefining possibilities for women everywhere.

In *Unleash Her: The Next Chapter Begins,* we are called to rise, transform, and continue breaking down barriers that have held us back. Our stories, filled with courage and resilience, become blueprints for future generations—proof that women are unstoppable forces of change.

Join the movement, unleash your potential, and together, let's write the next chapter of empowerment and transformation. Let's redefine what it means to be powerful women, inherently worthy of our dreams, and capable of inspiring lasting change.

Michelle Seguin

CEO of Peaceful Connections

https://www.linkedin.com/in/michelle-seguin-682806203/
https://www.facebook.com/peacefulconnections
https://www.peacefulconnections.ca/
https://www.largerthanlifepublishing.com/

Michelle Seguin is a 'Radical Recovery of Self' and 'Somatic Trauma-Informed' Coach, Speaker, Author, and Publisher who helps adults and teens heal from fibromyalgia, trauma, loss, and chronic pain. She guides clients through self-discovery and healing, helping them find peace and fulfillment by reconnecting mind and body. In 2013, Michelle experienced every parent's worst nightmare when her oldest son, Devin, unexpectedly passed away. Nothing could have prepared her for that depth of pain. Through lived experience and the study of healing modalities, she gained a deep understanding of how trauma impacts emotional and physical health. This opened her heart to helping others. Michelle is an engaging, passionate speaker who draws in her audience with insight into moving beyond trauma and leading a fulfilling life. Her understanding of trauma patterns and their effects allows her to gently guide others to their personal power and confidence through her open, loving presence.

The Day I Chose Me:
A Larger Than Life Awakening

By Michelle Seguin

For many women, there comes a real, soul-splitting moment when they realize they are living a life of quiet betrayals, not betrayals from others, though those do happen, but the ones they have committed against themselves. There are times when they said yes when their body screamed no. There are days when they smile while silently breaking. There are years when they poured from a cup that had been empty for so long that they forgot what it felt like to be full.

For me, that moment came in the still of a bed that I had barely left in two years. My body had become a battleground. Some days, the pain was so intense, so raw, so relentless that even turning on the TV was a challenge. When I tried to stand, a cold sweat would break out all over my body just from taking those first couple of steps. Some days, all I could do was lie curled in the fetal position in pain, tears streaming down my face, too exhausted to do anything but take that next breath. Fibromyalgia and chronic pain had taken over my body. I was depleted in a way that sleep could not fix. I wasn't just tired; I was done. I had nothing more to give as I had emptied my cup to the point of being unable to refill it.

I had become a shadow of the woman who once laughed and embraced life, who gave everything she had to everyone else until there was nothing left to give.

I remember that moment when everything came to a head. The question was so clear and felt so final that a decision needed to be made. It is time. It is time to decide. It is time to choose life or death. It was time to go be with my son Devin, who had passed once and for all, or it was time to fight for my life.

I didn't want to fight anymore. I was tired of the mess around me, tired of screaming into silence, trying to explain my grief to people who didn't get it. I was exhausted from trying to be someone I wasn't, from trying to please everyone around me, and from surviving.

Underneath all of that was the aching desire to be with my son. I just wanted to be with Devin. I wanted to feel his big arms wrap me in a bear hug. I wanted to lay my head on him and sob as he told me it would all be okay. I wanted to hear him say, "I love you, Mommy!!" when he knew I might get upset about something. I missed his laugh. I missed his voice. I missed him ensuring I knew I was an amazing mom. The grief of losing him, plus all of the other traumas I had experienced in life, consumed me. I didn't want to keep living like this.

As quickly as the thought of how easy it would be to fade off and be with my son, another part of me started to scream: *HOW DARE YOU. How dare you even consider taking the easy way out?* Devin never had the option to make the choice. He would have given anything to be here with his daughter. How could I be so selfish to consider the easy road? From deep within my soul, it all became clear to me. It was time to fight. I did not know how. I did not know when. I just knew that I had to start fighting.

That was the day I began to make a change in my life. I didn't start for me; I started for my two sons and granddaughter. I had to be strong for them, to show them what I was capable of. What I didn't realize or even consider at that time was that that choice was the very thing that would wake something up within me that I didn't even know existed.

Within days of this monumental moment, I had a spiritual awakening that changed everything. I went to bed, barely able to move; the pain was so intense. As I started to drift off, I heard a song playing, which was how Devin communicated with me. Then, the bright white light started enveloping me; I wasn't scared, but I was at peace. The next thing I knew, I was waking up the next morning. I got up and took two steps, and stopped instantly. Something significant had changed. The pain that was so intense the night before was now completely different. I felt completely different. I could finally move.

As the day progressed, I was suddenly drawn to meditations, affirmations, and anything that spoke to healing from a holistic standpoint. I wasn't just surviving anymore; I was being led. I was gaining strength with every step I took and every new tool I discovered. I didn't want to play small anymore. I wanted to live a life Larger Than Life, just like my son had. I had crystal-clear focus. I did not want my granddaughter to see me frail and fading. I wanted her to see me vibrant. I wanted to be a grandma who rode horses, jumped out of airplanes, and didn't think twice as she jumped on roller coasters with her.

The Road Back to Me

My healing journey was not a straight line. It came with twists and turns, ups and downs, and sometimes a few steps forward, then a few more steps backward. It came when I could only handle a small walk around my house. It came when I could only meditate for a minute or two. It came when I decided to do mirror work, and when I first looked at myself in the mirror, really looked at myself, I broke down in tears.

I saw the little girl who had endured abuse she should have never known to exist. That little girl had learned far too early that love came with conditions. That safety meant silence. That her needs did not matter; she had been abused before she could even understand what the word meant and had carried the pain like a second skin.

I saw the teenager who hated herself so much that she drank to blackout to escape the storm of emotions that were swirling within. I saw the mother, devastated and shattered, who had watched her son take his last breath. Every version of me stood in that mirror, layered atop the other. I wanted to look away, but I didn't. Something deep within knew that if I looked away, I would abandon her again.

That was the beginning of the sacred journey I was about to embark on. It was not self-love, at least not yet. The quiet, burning desire coming from my soul was telling me to fight for her, honor Devin, come home to myself, and be whole for the first time in decades.

I started by focusing on remembering to breathe. Next came the affirmations. At first, I could barely say them; I surely didn't believe them, but something told me to keep going. I started with simple affirmations like: I am safe. I am enough. I am worthy. When I began to say them, my inner critic became louder, even screaming. I was determined to shut that little voice up, whether it wanted to or not. I said these affirmations again and again. I sang them out loud so that my thoughts wouldn't have time to take over. Every time that little voice tried to take control, I said them repeatedly until it would finally stop.

Slowly, over time, my body began to soften. That inner voice got quieter and quieter. My mind became quiet, something I had never remembered being capable of. My soul began to exhale and feel at peace.

I was no longer the woman who always said yes. I was not the woman who over-functioned, over-gave, or over-explained. I was getting back to who I was at a soul level. I was getting back to the little girl who used to dream, who loved to laugh, who wanted to be held and told she was worthy and was enough.

I had never realized prior to that that I didn't even like myself, let alone love myself. I had been judging that girl my whole life. Criticizing her, abandoning her, shaming her.

Until that day when I looked in the mirror and whispered, "I see you. I'm sorry. I will not abandon you again. I love you."

Grief and the Cost of Silence

I didn't just grieve the trauma. I grieved the person I had become to survive it. The overachiever, the people pleaser, the one who could read a room better than she could read her own heart. I had to let her go. Thank her and set her free.

To do that, I started mapping my life on a timeline, pinpointing the traumas, limiting beliefs, and betrayals (especially the ones I allowed). I allowed myself to feel every bit: the shame, the heartbreak, the exhaustion. And then... I began to release it.

I did it through journaling, primal screams into a pillow, or letting the tears flow as needed until no tears were left. I used many trauma-release modalities. This wasn't just emotional work. It was bodywork. I learned that the disease in my body was not random; it was years of trapped emotions from trauma. Every "I'm fine" when I wasn't. Every "I can handle it" when I couldn't. Every bite of rage swallowed. Every desire buried, and every "no" that never left my lips. All of those choices had a cost, and I was done paying them.

Becoming Guru Mom

As I began to change, my relationships also began to shift. Some people celebrated the new me, while others did not. I started saying no, putting myself first, and speaking up, and this tended to rattle some people.

The difference was that now I understood that those who couldn't accept the new me were never meant to walk with me into this healed version of my life. I now live with boundaries. I live with a self-love that is untouchable. I know now that I don't need to shrink to keep people comfortable. I no longer need to tolerate those who prefer the broken version of me, the one they could walk all over. I deserve relationships that honor my wholeness, encourage my peace, and meet me in my light. Anything less is not love; it is control wearing a mask.

I will never forget the one night my youngest son was venting. He was angry, and I could feel myself getting pulled into the spiral like I had so many times before. But this time, I stayed centered. I looked at him and said, "As long as you keep thinking that way, that's what you will keep attracting."

He paused, blinked, and said, "Great, now I have to deal with guru mom."

I laughed because, yeah, I am guru mom now—the one who sees through the drama and projection, the one who has her own back, the one who knows who she is.

But don't get me wrong, it wasn't always clean. There were slips, and old patterns surfaced. There were moments when I caught myself back in over-giving, over-explaining, and over-functioning. I forgave myself, and I course-corrected. That is the difference now: I don't stay stuck.

What Standing in Your Power Feels Like

Standing in your power isn't glamorous; it is gritty. It is choosing yourself when everything in you wants to give in and make the chaos stop. There were times along the way when people around me pushed back hard. Gaslighting. Arguing. Manipulating. They tried so hard to drag me back into being the version of me that they could control, the one who made their lives easier by betraying my own. The tired, aching part of me just wanted to give in because the more I resisted, the more parts of my life fell apart. Deep down, I knew I would be gone forever if I chose them over me again. I would disappear for good, which Devin would not have wanted.

Devin wanted me to be alive and living Larger Than Life, like he had. He wanted me to embrace my granddaughter and become the wild, radiant, rollercoaster-riding grandma he would have imagined me to be. This knowledge helped me stay rooted. This was what standing in my power felt like.

Now, I check in with myself before making decisions. I always ask myself: *Is this my decision or someone else's expectation?* I no longer accept being treated like a convenience. I no longer twist myself into knots to be accepted. I know what I bring to the table and am no longer afraid to eat alone.

I love myself now. I love myself enough to walk away, to rest, to speak, to roar, to laugh, and to heal. The most beautiful part is that I am finally at peace, not because everything is perfect, but because I am aligned.

I no longer allow gaslighting, bullying, or guilt-tripping to dictate my choices. If someone can't respect my truth, then they no longer get access to my life.

To Every Woman Still Disappearing

To those women still disappearing in their lives, to those whose voice has gone quiet and whose needs feel like too much, I want you to hear this:

YOU DESERVE TO LIVE.

Not just to exist. Not just to survive. Not just to push through but to truly live. To laugh, dance, speak, dream, breathe, take up space. To be messy, to be bold, to be free.

You were not born to be small, to carry everyone else's pain, to break your heart to keep the peace. You are here to shine.

Your daughters and granddaughters need to see you empowered. Your sons and grandsons need to see you whole. Your inner child needs to see you choose her. And you... You need to feel what it is like to matter to yourself.

To the Girl I Was

If I could go back and sit beside the woman I used to be, the one curled up in pain, wondering if she would ever be okay, I would hold her hand and say: "You don't have to do it for them anymore. You get to do it for you. You don't have to be perfect. You have to begin. You have to choose yourself: one breath, one boundary, one truth at a time."

I would also look in her eyes and tell her: "I see you. I believe you. I will never leave you again."

And to the little girl in me who learned to stay quiet, to be small, I would whisper: "You were never the problem. You are enough. You are worthy. You are safe. You get to scream, sing, and live life fully."

My Invitation to You

This is an invitation to the tired, aching, and doubting woman reading this. It's your time now. Your next chapter begins the moment you say, "I choose me."

You don't have to be ready or fearless. You just have to be *willing*.

Willing to rest.
Willing to feel.
Willing to forgive.
Willing to begin again.

You don't need permission from anyone else. The only permission you need is your own. So take your life back.

Unleash her.

Let her rise.
Let her rest.
Let her roar.
Let her live.

Because she's been waiting for you.

Jenny Benitez

Founder of Steel Roses Women

https://www.linkedin.com/in/jenny-b-b1355433/
https://www.facebook.com/profile.php?id=61550731856422
https://www.instagram.com/steelrosespodcast/
www.steelroseswomen.com

Jenny Benitez is the creator and host of Steel Roses, a podcast built by women, for women. Each week, she brings raw, honest conversations to the forefront—tackling the unspoken pressures, struggles, and triumphs that shape women's lives. From motherhood and marriage to careers and personal identity, Jenny explores it all with transparency and heart. While being a mom doesn't define her entirely, it sparked a transformation that shaped her purpose: to support and uplift other women through shared experiences. Jenny knows firsthand what it's like to feel the weight of expectations and the isolation that often comes with them. That's why Steel Roses exists—to shed light on those silent struggles and give women a platform to be heard. Through every episode, Jenny stays rooted in her mission: to elevate women's voices, foster connection, and remind us all that we are not alone in the journey.

Empowering Women Through Authenticity: The Story of Steel Roses Podcast

By Jenny Benitez

Control, Alt, Delete

Writing this chapter has been difficult. What can I say that will inspire and empower other women? My story feels so ordinary, and yet in my core, I know that I have something important to share. I recently told someone I can look back on my life and identify three very distinct versions of myself, where pivotal moments took place that pushed me into the next version of me. What I find most interesting is that these pivotal moments were connected in some way to recentering myself through meditation, even though at the time, I didn't know this at all. It is a funny thing to have the pleasure to reflect back on your life, thinking through where you may have ended up had you taken different paths. The steadfast truth is that wherever you are in your life right now (whether you like it or not) was made possible by you. With the acceptance of this truth will come a great awakening: everything in your life was created by you, and thus you have the power to make significant changes. You just need the right tools and guidance to show you the way.

Setting the Stage for Burnout

I'll sleep when I'm dead. A mantra that defined my twenties and most of my thirties. The hustle culture had gripped me, and I was determined to "make it." Thinking back, I am not sure how much of my drive was because of what I thought I wanted and how much was because I was determined to prove everyone wrong. After a tumultuous time in my early twenties, I knew that the expectation was that I would not amount to anything great. I lost myself, lost my way, and wanted desperately to grasp onto something real. This marked the emergence of a powerful force within me that I would later learn was the ego part of me. This ego stepped up and took control, hard-nosed and severely driven. And so I dove, headfirst, into being everything that I *should* be. A career-driven workaholic, first one in the office and last one to leave, happily working 70+ hours a week. Desperate to climb the corporate ladder and willing to trash-talk my way into promotions, crushing whomever I needed to. You have time to eat your lunch? You must not be that busy. Let's give you more work. You leave the office at 5 p.m.? You must not be that dedicated to your job. Trial by fire was my life, and surviving it was a badge of honor. I clutched onto every word bestowed upon me by the more experienced women in the office, and the message was clear: You will get thrown in the deep end, so you better learn to swim.

What an odd training strategy, now in retrospect, as I reflect on my career, I realize how toxic some of the behaviors were. Managers focused on the negative, sink or swim, trial by fire, glorifying burnout culture, and encouraging gossip amongst team members. As I type this, I am shaking my head. How could anyone think that would be the best way to cultivate talent and good workplace habits? With every toxic experience, my armour would strengthen, but so would my resolve. At some point, I knew I would manage others, and when that time would come, I would remember something simple and yet incredibly important. Treat people how you want to be treated.

A pattern had started to emerge that, at the time, I did not recognize as a problem slowly poisoning my soul. With my ego in charge, the deep and unsettling need to control everything around me was overwhelming. Control would look different in various scenarios of my life, but it was always there. Professionally, it is presented as a "go-getter," someone willing to go that extra mile, stay late, and get the job done. I had very eagerly started my addiction to cortisol and dopamine by putting myself into intensely pressurized professional situations. My need to control sometimes presented itself as "supportive" to friends and family, but when you peel back the layers, the reality was that if I was being supportive, it was because I could control the outcome of the interaction. The person on the receiving end needed me, and that need satisfied a gaping hole inside of me that was created through the trauma of watching my parents' marriage disintegrate before my eyes many years before. It is amazing, really, our whole lives are shaped based on what we observed in our formative years. We all have a choice to take both the good and bad experiences into our adult lives and decide to make a change for the better.

The Lotus Flower

I sat staring at the ultrasound screen. "What is that small dark spot in the corner?" The ultrasound tech had confirmed what I already knew. Only 4 months after my son was born, I was pregnant again. As the tech shifted the wand, she gave my husband and me the surprising news that not only was I pregnant, but we were having twins. My mind raced as the technician relayed that one twin was quite small and may not make it to term. As we headed back to our one-bedroom apartment, reality hit me like a ton of bricks. How in the world would I be able to manage this? My son would be one year old by the time the twins were born. We were living in a very small apartment, bursting at the seams, and not in a good neighborhood. The tech had sufficiently frightened me that I could lose one of my twins, and oh yes, I was still working a full-time job. Developing my career was still a priority and had become more of a focal point after having my son. I was determined to do it all, up all night with an infant? Totally fine, I can still meet my deadline. High-risk twin pregnancy? Of course, I can still commute into NYC! Back-to-back meetings? I can eat on my walk to the conference room, and everything is fine! Yes, what had been ingrained in me early in my career, along with my ego desperate to control everything, continued to prevail. You better learn to swim, Jenny, or you will lose it all.

I was blessed in 2017 with twin girls, and with my one-year-old son in tow, I did what any working mom would do. I kept my head down and kept moving forward, surviving in a constant state of cortisol with little to no sleep. Looking back on that time now, I regret not slowing down and savoring the moment. I distinctly remember moments of resentment and, if I am honest, jealousy of other moms. They seemed to be enjoying all the milestones so much more, whereas I was constantly looking ahead to what needed to happen next. Bottle feeding? Over, let's get to solids. Tummy time? Head movement is strong; move on with crawling. The more independent they are, the better it is for me to be able to manage everything. And thus I set the tone for my children. Independence is crucial, and you want to learn how to do everything on your own. This way, I rationalized, you don't have to wait for Mommy all the time. My little crew nodded along as they learned how to make their own bowls of cereal, small snack trays, and clean their rooms. I often wonder if this was a mistake. Am I making my children independent? Or am I leading them down the same path I took, damning them to a fate of burnout.

From 2017 to 2021, I continued to push myself to handle it all. The ego part of me carried me through the development of my career and helped me continue my success while raising three infants. But one can only run at such a manic pace for so long. In 2020, I slowed down with the rest of the world during the pandemic. This was a catalyst moment for me where I had the full-time support of my husband and could, for the first time in years, prioritize my own health. I was desperately trying to lose all of the weight gained during my back-to-back pregnancies, and I received a crushing blow from my doctor. My constant state of cortisol, combined with 2–3 hours of sleep a night and my poor knowledge of nutrition and eating habits, had incapacitated my body and pushed me into a legitimate survival state. My body was prioritizing essential functions only, and compounded with my deprioritization of my own nutrition, there was no way I was going to get myself into shape. I had reached a critical mass point—depression wasn't just looming, it was nestling in for a long stay, and I had become uncomfortable in my own skin. I was embarrassed to leave the house and ashamed of how far I had let myself go. Sure, I could rationalize away why things had gone so far out of control. My plate was so full of everyone else's needs that I had no more room left for myself. How could I ever prioritize myself with three lives and a career in my hands?

The answer that I know now? Slowly. Many of us feel that we cannot make a change unless it is all at once and swift. That is the predominant reason why New Year's resolutions fail. Unless there is a life-threatening reason that change is needed, we as humans are unable to successfully make huge shifts. Our brains get used to living in a stressful state, with synapses firing constantly in the same patterns over and over again, making any big changes incredibly difficult. When you are trying to make a permanent change, you are quite literally rewiring your brain.

The concept of prioritizing myself was incredibly hard for me to wrap my head around. I was raised in a household that celebrated self-sacrifice and martyrdom. Sacrifice for your children, sacrifice for your husband, sacrifice to keep the peace, sacrifice to keep everyone happy...but at what point does this pattern begin to build resentment? And at what point will your needs ever be met? A terrible cycle permeated my life, allowing task after task to pile on me until I would blow. An inevitable screaming meltdown would take place, then wash, rinse, repeat.

While I was able to prioritize my health and get my physical body back on track, the cycle of burnout, allowing my ego to maintain control, stayed with me until summer 2022.

The Phoenix

The familiar ding of a virtual meeting starting snapped me out of my daydream. I was looking out the window of my home office. It was one of those gorgeous sunny days that brings droves of people to the beach, and I was inside watching as my husband and kids enjoyed the day. We made the decision to purchase a home in 2021 that fit our family needs with a great outdoor space and lots of room to grow. The first year was an overwhelming adjustment to say the least, which often led to me waking up in the middle of the night in a panic. *Do I deserve this blessing? Can I handle this? What if I lose it all?* And the usual *Who do you think you are? Everyone will find out you are a fraud.* Imposter syndrome is incredibly common for women to experience across all aspects of our lives, and becoming a homeowner was for me a hot zone of doubt. I knew that the anxiety I was experiencing wasn't real, and thus, every night I would engage in the dance of talking myself down from the ledge. By the light of day, my confidence would be somewhat restored, and my anxiety would refocus its attention to my daytime job. I held a position where I had the opportunity to lead by example and could put to use all of the lessons, good and bad, learned by my previous managers.

It is a rare occasion that I raise my hand and say, my plate is too full both professionally and personally. But this was one of those times in the early days of my awakening that I knew I had to speak up. In an effort to be better at my job, I was dipping my toe in the waters of setting boundaries. A painfully common issue I had was taking on too much and underestimating how much time things would take. I often found myself working late into the night and early the following morning to accomplish self-inflicted deadlines. Despite this, I was determined to be the manager that I always wished I had. If I wanted to break toxic work habits, then I too had to stop burning the midnight oil. And so, for the first time in my 15 years of experience, when a high-profile project was offered to me, I passed on taking the lead. I was already working above the standard 40-hour work week, and I knew that I couldn't take the project on without severely impacting my personal life.

Unfortunately, as is somewhat a common occurrence for many, the project found its way onto my plate anyway. In retrospect, no one forced it upon me, but after I formally passed on taking the lead, no one stepped up to the plate, and the team needed someone at the helm. You can call it ethics, professional responsibility, my ego rearing its ugly head, or just insanity, but I couldn't watch the team scramble without helping. And so I stepped up to the plate and for roughly three weeks, I was consumed. Waking up at 5 a.m. and working until well after my kids and husband had gone to bed. Only seeing my family at meal times and bath, and then hopping right back into work. Working from home is an incredible blessing. I know that the only reason I am able to manage my career and family life the way that I do is because I have this flexibility. But there is a darker side. Work never actually leaves you. When you commute, there is some decompression time before you transition to your role at home. There is also a buffer for leaving work at work. For me, there was no decompression, and there was no buffer. The lines of professional Jenny and mom/wife Jenny are often incredibly blurry, and in this particular instance, there were no lines.

So, what did I do? I put my blinders back on, put my head down, and plowed ahead, throwing everything at the wall and hoping that things would stick. By the end of the project, I was shaken, burnt out, and near tears from the stress and exhaustion. When I closed my laptop the day that the project was completed and stepped out of my office, I was relieved and felt accomplished. I had done it, I had completed the impossible project and still managed to pull off my duties as a mom and wife. And then it happened. My kids raced up to me as they always do when I am done with work to give me hugs and pepper me with kisses, "Mommy, are you *finally* done?!" they asked.

An overwhelming wave of emotion washed over me, and even as I type this a few years later, I can recall the feeling. I looked at their faces, and it hit me that I just lost three weeks of time with my children. They were bigger, their faces looked different, and as they pulled on my arms to come and play, my throat tightened and tears stung my eyes. It took only a few minutes for the revelation to hit me, but it was loud and clear: I will never lose time with them again for my career. In the grand scheme of things, regardless of how good I am at my job, I am just a number and replaceable. If I were to die tomorrow, my role would be filled within a few weeks, and the show would go on, but for my family, there would be a lifetime of loss. For my family, I am irreplaceable.

It felt like a shroud had been lifted from my head, and I was finally awake, for up until that moment, I was living my life full of "shoulds." For the first time, I was starting to think about what I really wanted from my life, and for those of you reading this that know me, when I make a decision to do something, I make it happen. So, I began making changes and found myself in a new role at another company. Same industry but at an agency that appeared to operate at a different pace, which would be more conducive to the work-life balance I was seeking. So, I prepared for a professional shift, and nearly simultaneously, I began the work of launching Steel Roses podcast. The desire to be an entrepreneur has always been with me, and in an effort to find balance and space from my professional life, podcasting felt like the right path. It was a no-brainer, really. I could meet and interview incredible women, and it didn't feel like something I should do; it felt like something I deeply wanted and needed to do for myself.

As with everything I decide to take on, a tremendous amount of research came first. How does one actually launch a podcast? With Google at my disposal, I dug deep looking for every resource I could that would help me bring a podcast into existence. The decision to launch a podcast did not come out of the blue. It was something I had talked about with my cousin from time to time over the course of several years. You see, as working moms, we found an incredible amount of connection in the struggles we were dealing with. Surely if both of us were experiencing these hurdles, others are, too, and wouldn't it be nice if a space existed that brought women together in a non-judgmental way to discuss the reality of being a woman in today's world? From this concept, Steel Roses Podcast came into existence and put me on the path of an incredible resource that would change the course of my life.

Now, I can look back and pinpoint exact moments where the Universe aligned and brought synchronicity to me. These moments are present for all of us, but many of us simply aren't listening. While cultivating resources to start my podcast, I came across a fellow podcaster who had a very successful online course. After engaging with her materials, I began to get the sense of something more, and for the first time in a very long time, I followed my instinct and I dove deeper. I invested in an intense three-month course that was designed to align me with my purpose. Now, I know what you may be thinking: These are a dime a dozen, they market big dreams, and it is total nonsense, you are throwing your money away. The woman leading the course had an incredibly successful podcast, and after listening to some of her episodes, I knew that she would be able to put me on the right path. What I wasn't expecting was everything else I learned. While podcasting was part of the course I was taking, so was the law of reception. The course expertly broke down into tangible steps exactly what one needed to do to unblock their flow with the universe in order to receive.

I already knew that I was ready for a change; I knew that I had gone far down the wrong path, and I was desperate to find a way to light myself up again. The very first incredibly powerful meditation that I participated in required me to acknowledge the different versions of myself that I had tucked away. This practice, if done correctly, unleashes a cascade of emotions that have been pent up for decades. This release is an essential step in unblocking your energy and making space for a tremendous amount of growth. This release opens up possibilities.

First, addressing little Jenny. She wanted to change the world. She was a force who was determined to help others. She wanted to volunteer in homeless shelters and help other kids. She was kind and wanted to bring peace to others. I imagined conversing with little Jenny. Explaining to her how far we have come, telling her that any sadness or frustration she was feeling would pass, and that she would be a success. But little Jenny wanted to be creative. She wanted to really live her life full of color and create something amazing. I gave little Jenny a hug and promised I would honor her. I had forgotten the pureness of just wanting to help others with no endgame in mind.

Second, addressing young adult Jenny. She lost her sense of self and was in the darkness. The family trauma she had internalized was a raging storm filling her with sadness, anger, and mistrust. She had no vision for her future and lived purely in the moment, looking externally to be saved. I embraced young adult Jenny, and the tears burst through like a dam that had been stopped up for decades. This Jenny needed to be shown softness. She needed to know that it was okay to let go of all of the hurt and to feel all of the emotions she had boxed up so long ago. Young adult Jenny no longer needed to hold up all the armor; she could finally let go and look to herself for peace.

And finally, mom and wife Jenny needed to know that she did not have to carry everything alone. She also needed to slow down and live in the moment. Savor the hugs, relish in the laughter, and recognize the miracle right before her eyes that she had worked hard for. It was time to release the ego part of me. While it saved me and helped to bring me to my present day, if I was ever going to live the life of my dreams, I needed to let go, live in the now, and be grateful.

This exercise, along with many other meditations, didn't just open doors; it blew away walls that I had structured in my mind throughout my entire life. From the teachings I experienced, I shifted the entire course of my life by simply letting my ego go and trusting in the flow and energy of the Universe around me. I reflect on the incredible changes that my life has gone through over the past few years since discovering the law of reception & meditation and I very easily identify examples all around me. There is a set of bushes in the front of my home that we intended to chop down as they were wildly overgrown when we moved in. Upon further investigation when we began cutting the bushes back we noticed that there were actually 3 distinct bushes, two green shrubs and one rose bush that had been choked down to a single stem by the two shrubs. My husband and the landscaper insisted we remove the rose bush. They rationalized, it's a single stem, it won't survive, it looks ugly, we can replace it with a new bush. But I saw more, so I asked that the two shrubs be trimmed and provide space for my single rose stem. I have kept an eye on this single rose stem over the course of a year and in the spring I saw the first signs of life beginning to sprout from this single stem. After several weeks the branches protruding from the single stem have doubled and grown stronger so I trimmed the hedges back even more and have provided support to this rose bush to continue its growth. This rose bush represents all of us. This rose bush represents me, once upon a time, not so long ago, my spirit, my soul was slowly dying as it was choked by the onslaught of pressure and tasks and roles I kept taking on. I was only saved when I started to let things fall away, in some instances cut away, to allow myself to breathe, be in the moment, and thrive. Only then, has my true happiness come into existence. Only now can I truly, authentically say that I am living the life of my dreams.

Fernanda Lima Firman

Brezze.AI
Architect of Automated Success

https://www.linkedin.com/in/felimafirman/
https://www.facebook.com/fefirman/
https://www.instagram.com/fernanda.firman/
https://www.fernandafirman.com/
https://crm.brezze.ai/

Fernanda Lima Firman, a Brazilian architect turned AI Marketing and Automation Strategist, is the powerhouse behind multiple 6-figure launches that have revolutionized how her clients grow without burnout. As founder of Brezze.ai, she transforms struggling businesses into profit machines with AI-powered systems and custom ChatGPT assistants that eliminate manual chaos, saving clients 15+ hours weekly while increasing conversion rates. In today's AI-driven market, businesses without intelligent automation are being left behind. Fernanda bridges this critical gap by implementing systems that handle everything from client acquisition to fulfillment automatically. Her proprietary Profit Architecture™ Blueprint, proven across 50+ events (summits, giveaways, launches, workshops), enables clients to generate high-quality leads, build unshakeable authority, and convert on autopilot while selling digital products, courses, and memberships. Fernanda's mission: empower her clients to monetize their expertise without burnout and to be the architect of their automated success. She equips them with AI-powered foundations that boost sales while reducing operational stress by 80%, transforming overwhelm into organized, profitable success.

Built to Rise: How I Reinvented My Life and Business at 50 with Faith, AI, Systems, and Strategy

By Fernanda Lima Firman

1. Releasing the Old Blueprint: Who Am I Now?

I wasn't just tired, I felt an emptiness deep within me. Not from motherhood, which I had joyfully chosen alongside my loving husband, Eric, but from the emotional weight of leaving a career I had spent decades building.

For most of my adult life, I have been an architect, a woman of plans, precision, and purpose. I knew how to design buildings that stood the test of time, but no blueprint had ever taught me how to redesign a life that looked perfect on the outside but felt disconnected on the inside.

From the outside, everything looked like a masterpiece. I had built a fulfilling career with a renowned architect in San Diego, designing high-end, custom homes that reflected precision and dreams. My projects were celebrated, my skills trusted. Yet inside, I felt the quiet stirring of a different kind of design calling. There was no failure, no collapse, no burnout—only a divine interruption. A knowing. A whisper I couldn't ignore. Something sacred had shifted.

At nearly 47, life seemed complete: a beautiful home, a loving family, two healthy sons, conceived despite being told I was too old, and a career I had spent years mastering. And yet, something within me had already begun to unravel and reshape. The strong voice I used to lead teams and present bold designs began to quiet, making space for something new.

I asked a close friend to describe me as if introducing me to someone new. She spoke of my creativity, energy, and fire, but never once mentioned that I was an architect. That silence said everything. My identity had already shifted; my voice was leading somewhere new.

When I finally told the architect I was ready to step away, she simply looked at me and said, "I know... I've been feeling the shift in you." That moment was my confirmation. I was being called to something else entirely.

The joy I once found in design hadn't vanished; instead, it had simply evolved into a new understanding. At that moment, I knew: This season was complete. In that unexpected silence, the question echoed:

What if I wasn't meant to follow the old blueprint anymore?

What if I was meant to design an entirely different one?

When I made this pivotal decision, I had no plan. No job lined up. Nothing was perfectly in place. Just a nudge. A knowing. A sacred leap of faith.

2. The Unseen Foundation: Laying New Groundwork

Long before the pandemic changed the world, I had started helping Eric with his business. As a healthy home contractor, his services were in demand, but his systems were stuck in manual mode. I saw an opportunity not just to support him, but the feeling of building a family business.

The first event I planned for his business gave us an email list of over a thousand potential clients and warm leads who were ready to take action. It positioned us in front of industry leaders and sparked unexpected partnerships. Our message about detoxing homes landed with clarity, and I saw how my gifts could create momentum in ways I hadn't before.

My goal was not to start a business on my own. But I couldn't ignore how alive I felt when simplifying chaos, creating clarity, and bringing strategy to the table. That inner pull led me to invest seriously, over $100,000 in coaching programs.

I wasn't chasing trends; I was leveraging wisdom. At my age, I knew time was too valuable for free tutorials or shallow content. So, I searched for elite coaches who could see my business clearly, offer strategy, and guide me to the results I needed fast. I hired experts in marketing, automation, client experience, systems design, and AI. Everything I learned I implemented immediately.

Inside those coaching programs, I noticed something significant: the women, especially those over 40, were overwhelmed by tech, confused by their messaging, and paralyzed by too many moving parts. I began helping from the heart, offering clarity, mapping their launches, cleaning up their backends, and building workflows. I wasn't selling anything, I was simply doing what I've always done: seeing the 3D structure of their business, creating flow, and building toward a clear vision.

It felt natural, like mentoring junior architects in my past career. However, the results these women experienced were remarkable. They weren't just learning new skills; they were gaining confidence and clarity. That's when I realized my strategic mind, the one that had thrived in architecture, was perfectly suited for business building. I wasn't starting from scratch but translating what I already knew into a new context.

3. Crisis to Clarity: The Client Who Sparked My New Chapter

Then, the world shut down. Eric's business stalled, and I became a homeschool mom overnight, as our income paused.

Confined yet seeking connection and purpose in this new reality, I participated in a virtual event hosted by Tony Robbins. During a breakout session, while sharing launch strategies, one woman kept returning for further insights. Eventually, she posed the pivotal question: "Can I hire you?" And just like that, I secured my first $5,000 client, all without a website, a formal pitch, or even an official offer.

My business was born not through a funnel, but through generosity, clarity, and presence.

It is clear that my training as an architect has prepared me for this. I see the big picture while managing the tiniest details; I can translate vision into structure, and chaos into flow. Now, instead of designing homes, I was designing strategy, systems, and client journeys.

4. Systems and Strategy: The Architecture of My Business

In the beginning, I did what many entrepreneurs do: I said yes to everything. I mapped launch plans, built funnels, created email sequences, and personally supported every client from beginning to end. I wanted to give women the clarity they had been missing, but very quickly, the weight of doing it all myself began to show.

My client base grew fast, but without support, I quickly became the bottleneck. This wasn't like my architecture days, where I had systems and a team. Now, I needed a way to serve more clients without losing myself.

That's when I returned to what I knew: vision, design, structure, and flow. So, I created systems, not just for my clients, but for myself. I automated, optimized, and leveraged AI whenever I could. And I built what I now call the architecture of my business.

Just as I had done for years in architecture, I began to see the challenges in 3D. In the same way, I used to spot design flaws in a blueprint before it became a problem on-site, and I saw the bottlenecks in women's businesses that were stopping their growth. And just like that, because I had fixed my own bottleneck, I was able to fix theirs as well.

One of my turning points was launching CRM, Brezze, a business platform powered by AI that offers my clients tools to automate lead nurturing, scheduling, campaign tracking, and customer journeys. I followed that with Brezze.AI, our AI-powered receptionist that now books calls 24/7, pre-qualifies leads, answers client questions, and even closes some sales.

The real sense of freedom came when I trained my ChatGPT, my business partner now, to think and write like me.

These tools save me, and my clients, 10 or more hours a week. That time is now invested in what matters most: people, strategy, and legacy.

And something beautiful began to happen.

I watched women, many over 45, who once felt intimidated by technology, launch their offers with confidence. They started generating income while spending more time with their families. They stopped spinning in circles and started moving with clarity.

Each time a client succeeded, I felt something deep within me shift. It wasn't just about building a business; it was about becoming part of their ripple. Because when they grew, their work touched others. Their income grew. Their impact multiplied. And I knew: I had helped make that possible.

That sense of accomplishment didn't come from income or recognition; it came from seeing women reclaim their voice and finally say yes to dreams they'd buried for years.

5. The REWIRE™ Method: Your Framework for Unstoppable Growth

As I worked with more women, I started to notice a pattern: they were missing their blueprint. Reinvention wasn't just about mindset or marketing; it required rewiring how we see ourselves and how we run our businesses.

I met many women who, like me, wanted to leave the corporate world, not because they lacked ambition, but because they craved a sense of presence. They didn't want to choose between impact and motherhood. They wanted a business that fit into their life, not one that consumed it, leaving them depleted. These were smart, capable women who had built successful careers, yet still felt something was missing: a deep resonance, a sense of true alignment between who they were and what they were doing.

They wanted freedom, alignment, and a life they didn't need to escape from.

That's how the REWIRE™ framework was born. It's the same path I took, and it's now the path I guide my clients through, acting as their strategic mentor every step of the way:

- **R**ecognize where you are now without guilt, shame, or comparison, finally liberating yourself from self-judgment and pinpointing the true bottlenecks holding your vision back.

- **E**mbrace your strengths, your season, your experience—and honor your timeline, stepping fully into your authentic power and unearthing the unique expertise that will fuel your courses and community.

- **W**eave your story, your voice, and your values into a message that connects, magnetizing your ideal audience and crafting a compelling narrative for your courses and brand community.

- **I**ntegrate systems, automation, and AI that support your energy and purpose, gaining effortless efficiency and renewed energy by designing the digital architecture for your courses, client journeys, and community management.

- **R**ebuild your business with strategy and intention, not burnout, designing a venture that truly serves your life and structuring your offers, from courses to community platforms, for sustainable growth.

- **E**xpand with collaboration and focus so your revenue, your reach, and your rest grow together, living a life of expansive impact and profound well-being as you leverage AI to amplify your efforts and scale your course and community impact.

Reinvention isn't about erasing what came before. It's about using everything you've lived, learned, and led to build something even more aligned. That's what this framework allows. And it's what I believe every woman, especially mothers over 40, deserves to access.

6. Built to Rise: Your Next Chapter Is Now

This journey of building on your past with intention, wisdom, and courage is precisely what it means to rise.

My past, like yours, shaped every part of this journey.

I've been underestimated more times than I can count. And yet, I've never believed in expiration dates. Only divine timing.

I was told I was too old to have children. I had my sons at 39 and 42, after 3 miscarriages, and everyone was saying I was too old to carry a pregnancy.

About 20 years ago, I left an abusive marriage and fled to a shelter in Los Angeles. When he found me there, the shelter had to let me go. I was transferred to San Diego: homeless, with nothing but faith. I rebuilt and healed. San Diego is where I met my husband.

When I left Brazil, I was almost done with my master's degree. Here in America, many had said I was "no one" and that I was wasting my time trying to finish it. They said it would never happen to me here. But after many hurdles, fueled by quiet defiance, I not only finished but proudly earned my master's degree, a powerful affirmation of my lifelong commitment to my vision, regardless of external doubts.

Back when I first came to America at 23, I worked as a house cleaner and babysitter, jobs I deeply respect. But I was told that was all I'd ever do. At 31, I proved otherwise. I came to America to work as an architect and built something bigger, brick by brick, system by system.

My name, *Fernanda*, means "bold journey," "adventure," and "courage," a declaration I was born to live.

For a few years, I carried that meaning quietly, rooted in a confidence that had long defined me. But during the pandemic, facing no income for my husband and me, with two young sons and a house to pay for, a chilling fear crept in, momentarily dimming that inner fire. I stepped away from the bold spirit of my name then. Yet, when I stopped trying to fit back into an old blueprint and instead embraced who I was becoming, I finally felt it again! Fully.

My name was never just something I answered to. It was a declaration I was born to live, a destiny I was finally stepping into.

So, if you're standing at a crossroads, unsure whether to leap... Let this be your sign.

You don't need to burn it all down to begin again. You don't need to hit rock bottom. You don't need permission.

You need a system. You need support. And most of all, you need to believe that the next version of your life isn't late, it's right on time.

Because you're not starting from scratch. You're starting from wisdom.

She's not waiting. She's unleashed. And she's already rising.

Free Resources: www.fernandafirman.com/Ai4Biz

☞ AI Resources: Prompts, AI assistants

☞ Systems Quizz

☞ Watch my free training "AI For Business" to uncover how you can integrate AI, systems, and automation, reclaim your time, and rebuild something sustainable to build a business that supports your life, not one that takes over it.

Kimberly Tyler

https://www.linkedin.com/in/kimberly-tyler-a8849539/
https://www.facebook.com/profile.php?id=100094747320115
https://www.instagram.com/kimmijotyler/
https://www.brokenvesselholylight.com/

Kimberly Tyler, M.Ed, is an international best-selling author with over 30 years in education and children's ministry leadership. A retired Education Director and dedicated teacher, she possesses a wealth of knowledge and experience in student success through positive learning environments and advocating for inclusive practices. Kimberly is an inspiring author with a profound gift for seeing others succeed despite any challenges that they may face. Residing in Northern California with her husband and extended family, she draws inspiration from the beautiful surroundings and close-knit community. Kimberly's writing reflects her genuine desire to uplift and empower readers as she shares stories that resonate with faith, hope, and resilience. Her unique blend of storytelling and encouragement has positively impacted the hearts of readers worldwide. An accomplished creative, her favorite mediums are fabric arts such as quilting and embroidery.

Confidence with a Purpose: The Proverbs 31 Woman as a God-Assured Businesswoman

By Kimberly Tyler

Have you ever looked at the Proverbs 31 woman and thought, "I could never be like her?" I know I have. She seems to do it all—manages her home, runs a thriving business, keeps her family happy, clothed, and fed, and still has time to speak wisdom and kindness to everyone around her. It's easy to read that passage and feel overwhelmed, maybe even a little discouraged. But here's what I've come to realize: She isn't a picture of perfection—we were never meant to read her that way. She's a picture of "purposeful confidence." And that confidence? It doesn't come from how capable she is—it comes from how connected she is to God.

The Proverbs 31 woman is a confident businesswoman, but her confidence isn't self-made. It's God-given. She's bold and strategic because she walks in step with the Lord. She makes wise decisions not because she knows everything but because she trusts the One who does. She shows us that real confidence—the kind that lasts—is born in faith, nurtured in trust, and lived out in love. It's amazing that we have that kind of confidence available to us as well.

Rooted in God: The Source of Her Confidence

Let's begin at the foundation. Proverbs 31:30 says, *"Charm is deceitful, and beauty is passing, but a woman who fears the Lord, she shall be praised."* That verse is the heartbeat of the entire passage. Everything she does—every decision, every task, every act of kindness—flows from this reverent relationship with God.

When we think about confidence, the world tells us it comes from how we look, what we've accomplished, or how many followers we have.

But this woman knows better. Her assurance isn't rooted in external things. She doesn't need validation from people to feel valuable. She has found her identity in the Lord—and that changes everything.

Her fear of the Lord isn't a fear that shrinks back; it's a deep respect, a surrendered awe that leads to wisdom, strength, and clarity. It's not a burden—it's a blessing. She doesn't waste energy trying to prove herself because she knows she's already approved by the One who matters most.

And that's the kind of confidence we're invited into. Not the kind that puffs us up or puts on a show, but the kind that whispers, *Even when I don't have all the answers, I know the One who does.* It's steady. It's unshakable. And it's available every day we choose to walk closely with God.

When our confidence is rooted in Him, we no longer live to impress—we live to express His goodness through our lives. That's a firm foundation, one worth building every area of our life and business upon.

It's also worth noting that the Proverbs 31 woman didn't grow this confidence overnight. It was cultivated daily—through prayer, obedience, and learning to listen for God's voice in every area of her life. Her relationship with God wasn't a side note—it was the anchor. And that's good news for us because it means we don't have to strive to be confident—we simply have to stay connected to the One who fills us with it.

She Plans, She Builds, She Trades: A Strategic Entrepreneur

If anyone tells you the Bible doesn't talk about women in business, just point them to Proverbs 31. This woman is not only spiritual and nurturing—she's also sharp, savvy, and strategic. Look at verses 16, 18, and 24:

"She considers a field and buys it; from her profits, she plants a vineyard... She perceives that her merchandise is good... She makes linen garments and sells them and supplies sashes for the merchants."

She's a planner. She studies the field before buying it. She reinvests her profits to create something even more fruitful. She recognizes the value of her work and doesn't hesitate to bring it to market. This is not passive faith—this is active, purposeful confidence lived out through smart decisions and God-led entrepreneurship.

It's encouraging to see that faith and business are not at odds in this passage—they're intertwined. Her relationship with God empowers her to make wise investments, build wealth, and provide for her family and others. That's the beauty of walking with the Lord: He doesn't just care about our hearts; He cares about our hands and what we do with them.

Whether you're selling handmade goods from your kitchen table, launching an online store, or leading a corporate team, your work matters. And when you surrender your plans to God, you can move forward boldly, knowing He is your guide and provider.

Strength and Dignity: Her Character Is Her Branding

Proverbs 31:25 says, "Strength and honor are her clothing; she shall rejoice in time to come." In today's terms, you could say her character is her brand. She wears strength and dignity like a well-tailored outfit. And just like clothing, it's something she puts on intentionally.

What stands out is that her strength isn't loud—it's steady. Her dignity doesn't scream for attention—it speaks through her actions. She doesn't rely on flashy marketing or performance. Her confidence comes from knowing she's doing what God called her to do and doing it with integrity.

We live in a world that often confuses confidence with arrogance. But the Proverbs 31 woman reminds us that true confidence doesn't push others down—it lifts them up. She doesn't need to compare or compete. She knows who she is and who she is, and that alone gives her peace.

You and I can walk in that same peace. We don't have to be the loudest or the most polished. When we clothe ourselves in godly strength and dignity, it becomes our testimony. It shows up in how we speak, serve, and do business—with grace and purpose.

She Leads with Wisdom and Kindness

One of my favorite verses in the whole chapter is Proverbs 31:26: "She opens her mouth with wisdom, and on her tongue is the law of kindness." Isn't that beautiful? This woman doesn't just lead with her hands—she leads with her words.

She's not harsh or domineering. She doesn't run her home or business with fear. Instead, she leads from a place of wisdom and kindness. That doesn't mean she's weak. On the contrary, it takes a strong woman to lead with grace. It takes true confidence to correct gently, to speak the truth in love, and to offer kindness when it's not required.

As women in business, we can sometimes feel pressure to be harsh or aggressive to earn respect. But the Proverbs 31 woman shows us a better way. She's respected not because she's hard, but because she's wise and kind.

Let's be those kinds of leaders. Let's run our businesses and lead our homes with the wisdom that comes from God and the kindness that reflects His heart.

Her Confidence Impacts Generations

Proverbs 31:27-28 says, "She watches over the ways of her household, and does not eat the bread of idleness. Her children rise up and call her blessed; her husband also, and he praises her."

This isn't just about productivity—it's about legacy. Her confidence, her business, her leadership—they all have ripple effects. Her children are watching. Her community is impacted. Her husband sees the fruit of her labor and praises her.

And that's the bigger picture: her work is not just about income. It's about influence. She's building something that lasts, blesses others, and points back to the God she serves.

That's the kind of confidence we're called to—one that goes beyond our own success and touches the lives of those around us. Whether you're raising babies or building brands, your faith-fueled confidence matters. And it doesn't just change your story—it changes generations.

Walking in God's Confidence

The Proverbs 31 woman isn't some superhero we have to strive to become. She's a woman who simply walks closely with God—and that closeness becomes her confidence.

Her strength isn't in her schedule or her sales. Her confidence isn't rooted in her looks or her bank account. It's rooted in her relationship with the Lord.

And friend, you and I are invited into that same kind of confidence. A confidence that plans wisely, speaks kindly, leads with integrity, and impacts generations—all because we're leaning on God every step of the way.

So, let's let go of perfection and lean into purpose. Let's run our businesses, our homes, and our lives with the assurance that comes from knowing we are called, we are equipped, and we are never alone.

Here's the beautiful truth: Confidence doesn't begin with achievement—it begins with alignment. When our hearts are aligned with God's Word, when our plans are surrendered to His wisdom, and when His Spirit guides our efforts—we can step forward with bold, holy confidence. Not only will our lives be transformed, but so will the lives of those around us.

So start today. Start small if you must. But start knowing this: you are capable, you are called, and with God's strength, you are already equipped. Walk forward in faith—your confidence is safe in His hands.

JOIN THE MOVEMENT!
#BAUW

Becoming An Unstoppable Woman
With She Rises Studios

She Rises Studios was founded by Hanna Olivas and Adriana Luna Carlos, the mother-daughter duo, in mid-2020 as they saw a need to help empower women worldwide. They are the podcast hosts of the *She Rises Studios Podcast* and Amazon best-selling authors and motivational speakers who travel the world. Hanna and Adriana are the movement creators of #BAUW - Becoming An Unstoppable Woman: The movement has been created to universally impact women of all ages, at whatever stage of life, to overcome insecurities, and adversities, and develop an unstoppable mindset. She Rises Studios educates, celebrates, and empowers women globally.

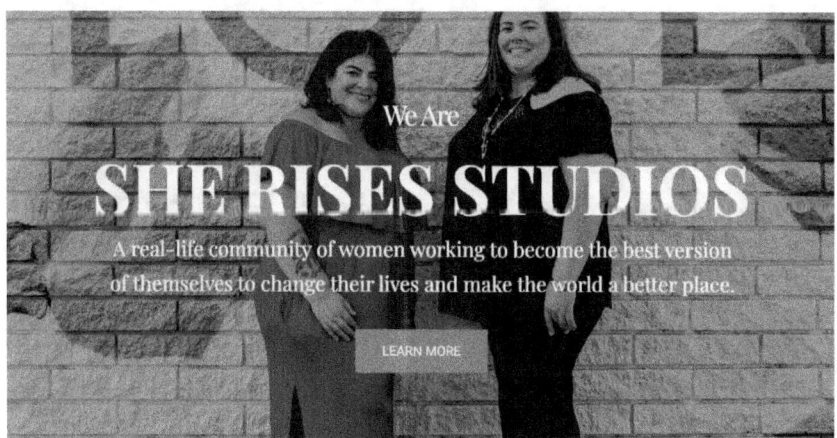

Looking to Join Us in our Next Anthology or Publish YOUR Own?

She Rises Studios Publishing offers full-service publishing, marketing, book tour, and campaign services. For more information, contact info@sherisesstudios.com

We are always looking for women who want to share their stories and expertise and feature their businesses on our podcasts, in our books, and in our magazines.

SEE WHAT WE DO

OUR PODCAST   **OUR BOOKS**   **OUR SERVICES**

Be featured in the Becoming An Unstoppable Woman magazine, published in 13 countries and sold in all major retailers. Get the visibility you need to LEVEL UP in your business!

Have your own TV show streamed across major platforms like Roku TV, Amazon Fire Stick, Apple TV and more!

Learn to leverage your expertise. Build your online presence and grow your audience with FENIX TV.
https://fenixtv.sherisesstudios.com/

Visit www.SheRisesStudios.com to see how YOU can join the #BAUW movement and help your community to achieve the UNSTOPPABLE mindset.

Have you checked out the *She Rises Studios Podcast?*

Find us on all MAJOR platforms: Spotify, IHeartRadio, Apple Podcasts, Google Podcasts, etc.

Looking to become a sponsor or build a partnership?

Email us at info@sherisesstudios.com

www.ingramcontent.com/pod-product-compliance
Lightning Source LLC
Chambersburg PA
CBHW071326120626
46546CB00002B/457